T0289427

RAND

Encouraging Recruiter Achievement

A Recent History of Military Recruiter Incentive Programs

Carole Oken, Beth J. Asch

Prepared for the
Office of the Secretary of Defense
United States Army

National Defense Research Institute
Arroyo Center

PREFACE

In the spring of 1994, the Army Chief of Staff and the Deputy Secretary of Defense asked RAND to examine recent trends in the recruiting market and assess their implications for meeting accession requirements. The request for assistance came about because of indications of increased difficulty in meeting recruiting goals. It consisted of two parts: (1) a quick initial examination of the trends and (2) a longer-term research agenda to study the recruiting outlook in depth. The results of the preliminary examination were briefed in May 1994 and are described in MR-549-A/OSD, *Recent Recruiting Trends and Their Implications: Preliminary Analysis and Recommendations* (Asch and Orvis, 1994).

This report presents results from the longer-term analysis. In it we describe recruiter incentive plans in each service and how they have changed over time. Its findings should interest planners and policymakers concerned with recruiting. Additional results from the longer-term analysis are described in MR-677-A/OSD, *Military Recruiting Outlook: Recent Trends in Enlistment Propensity and Conversion of Potential Enlisted Supply* (Orvis, Sastry, and McDonald, 1996) and other documents that will be forthcoming as part of this project.

This research was conducted within the Manpower and Training Program, part of RAND's Arroyo Center, and within the Forces and Resources Policy Center, part of RAND's National Defense Research Institute. The Arroyo Center and the National Defense Research Institute are both federally funded research and development centers, the first sponsored by the United States Army and the second by the Office of the Secretary of Defense, the Joint Staff, and the defense agencies.

CONTENTS

TABLES

SUMMARY

Even before accession requirements began rising in FY96, military recruiters reported some difficulty meeting accession goals during the enlisted-force drawdown, which bottomed out in FY94-95. Using two approaches, RAND examined the supply of potential recruits in the spring of 1994 and concluded that the pool of high-quality youth was adequate to meet DoD's needs. If anything, more potential recruits were available relative to accession needs than before the drawdown.

Could changes in recruiting practices explain the accession difficulties? As one step toward answering this question, we reviewed the evolution over the last 15 to 20 years of recruiter incentive plans in each of the services. In this report, we present this review in considerable detail, service by service, for enlisted personnel in the active force. (The review concentrates on national-level plans; the service recruiting commands also allow their various subordinate jurisdictions to establish plans.) Here, we look across the services in an effort to arrive at some generalizations.

Every year, each service's recruiting command sets accession goals that will allow it to meet a congressionally mandated "end strength" with a desirable experience profile. These goals may also include subsidiary objectives for recruits of high aptitude or with certain skills or other characteristics. The goals are allocated down a hierarchy of organizational elements within the recruiting command, e.g., regions, districts, and stations. Through the 1980s, all services also set goals for individual recruiters. Since FY90, however, the Navy has operated without individual goals, and the Army has since followed suit although the Army recently began using individual goals again. Both those services relied on team goals as incentives for individuals. The Air Force and Marine Corps continue to set goals for individual recruiters.

Each recruiting command has a system of awards for the top-performing units or individuals (or both). These range from plaques and other mementos to achievement medals and enhanced promotion opportunities. Award candidates are nominated by commanders at various levels, based largely on objective performance measures, with some attention to various subjective factors. Performance is measured objectively by the number of recruiting contracts written over some period of time. Within these general parameters, incentive plans at the national level have differed among services in important ways. While it is difficult to neatly classify the plans into simple categories, Table S.1 provides a general summary that attempts to do so.

- *Primary Emphasis.* Though all services have ways of rewarding both units and individuals, the emphasis differs. Until recently the Army's emphasis has been on individual awards (toward which unit performance counts), whereas the Marine Corps emphasizes unit awards. The Air Force and Navy reward both units and individuals.

- *Eligibility Basis.* Awards can be given either for attaining certain criteria (i.e., absolute performance) or for coming out at or near the top in a competition (relative performance). Army recruiters and Marine recruiting units are eligible for awards on achievement of specified criteria--a point total attained or a set of goals fulfilled in a given period of time. That is also true of one of the Navy plans and of the Air Force's plan for individual incentives. But the Air Force unit incentive plan and one of the Navy plans have used competition or relative performance as a stimulus. In such a plan, award eligibility goes to the individual or unit with the top point total or the highest number of recruits of a particular type secured, over some geographical area and time period.

In addition to the cross-service variation in incentive plans, these plans have also evolved significantly within most of the services during the 1990s. The Navy added to one of its individual-incentive plans a component that awarded "team play" by allowing individuals to take credit for achievements by their unit. The Army already had such a provision but expanded it. The Navy took one of its plans off a point system and put the other one on. It then devolved authority for the

Table S.1

Summary Characteristics of National-Level Service Recruiting Plans

Service and Plan	Years in Effect	Primary Emphasis[a]	Eligibility Basis[b]
Army			
Program 300	FY82 - FY94	Individual/ unit	Absolute
Success 2000	FY95 - FY97	Unit	Absolute
Navy			
Freeman Plan	FY79 - FY88	Individual	Absolute
Competition System	FY79 - FY90	Unit	Relative
Recruiter Meritorious Advancement Program	FY90 - FY93	Individual	Relative
Recruiter Advancement Through Excellence program	FY90 - FY93	Unit	Relative
Quality-Incentive-System-based competition[c]	FY90 - FY94	Unit	Relative
Recruiter Excellence Incentive Program	FY93 - present	Individual/ unit	Relative
Air Force			
Competition System	Early 1970s to FY93, FY95[d]	Unit	Relative
Awards Program[e]	Early 1970s to present	Individual	Mixed
Marine Corps			
National Plan[f]	Late 1970s to present	Unit	Mixed

[a]"Individual" indicates emphasis on incentives for individual recruiters; "unit" indicates emphasis on unit incentives.

[b]"Absolute" indicates that award eligibility rests on achieving specified numbers; "relative" indicates that eligibility depends on achieving better numbers than others achieve.

[c]The basis for the Navy Competition System changed to QIS in FY90. A national-level system terminated in FY94; most lower-level commands still use a QIS-type system.

[d]In FY94, groups and their associated squadrons designed unique competition systems rather than a national system.

[e]The Air Force Awards Program also issues awards to units based on Competition System totals.

[f]The Marine Corps depends on lower commands to create and manage competition and awards plans in addition to the national plan.

second system to lower levels in the command structure. The Air Force also devolved authority for its unit award system for one year, then reinstated it at the national level. The Marine Corps, whose national-level award system has been modest in scope compared to the others, has all along had strong incentive programs at lower levels. These programs have shown almost as much diversity as that exhibited across services.

The diversity we observe across service incentive plans and over time may be due to various causes, including service culture and changes associated with the drawdown. We know that some of the changes arose from judgments of misalignment between service goals and unit and individual goals induced by incentives, or from concerns over fairness across recruiters. Some of the changes also represent responses to problems in attaining accession objectives at some levels within the service. But the variety of changes suggest that, in general, the services have been struggling over time to find the best incentive plan to fit their needs.

To understand what the best incentive plan is for each service and what its features would be, one first needs a framework or model of how recruiters respond to alternative incentive plan features. In addition, one needs empirical estimates of how alternative features affect recruiter behavior. Unfortunately, both are lacking. Past work in these areas (for example, Dertouzos, 1985; Asch, 1990; and Asch and Karoly, 1993) tends to narrowly focus on either setting and achieving goals or on specific groups of recruiting personnel in specific locations. Future research needs to take a broader approach. In providing background on the incentive plans and how they have changed over time, this report lays the groundwork for such research.

ACKNOWLEDGMENTS

Acquiring the extensive historic and contemporary documents and other information necessary to review recruiter incentive systems for all four military service branches required the assistance of numerous recruiting specialists within the services, at other organizations, and at RAND. Their job was made even more difficult because so many documents were destroyed in compliance with the Paperwork Reduction Act. In addition to providing printed materials, several people patiently and thoughtfully spoke with us explaining and illuminating their incentive and awards programs documentation, and reviewed our draft report for their service branch.

Our primary Army contact at Headquarters United States Army Recruiting Command, Sergeant First Class Michael Ayers, generously updated materials we had acquired for previous studies and provided valuable insights about the way army recruiters respond to incentives and the way incentives have changed in response to recruiting practices. Sergeant Ayers was a member of the team that developed the recently instituted Success 2000 incentive and awards program.

We extend our gratitude to Dr. Edward Schmitz and Mr. Carl Kannapel at the Research Studies Branch of the Research Division, Commander, Navy Recruiting Command (CNRC), and to several members of the CNRC staff including Ed Kearl on goals and Kate Peerman on the Quality Incentive System. They supplied extensive documentation and graciously, in great detail, discussed the evolution of the current recruiter incentive system. They also spent substantial time helping to increase our understanding of the various incentive programs. In addition, Ravi Sharma at the Center for Naval Analyses (CNA) discussed differences between current and past incentive systems and helped us obtain historic documents at CNA.

At the Air Force Recruiting Service Headquarters, George Germadnik provided information about goals and guided us through the system. Master Sergeants Darryl Casey and Ron Attaquin and Chief Master Sergeant Gregory McCord provided the necessary documentation and responded to our many inquiries about the competition, incentive award, and goaling systems. Their experience and knowledge benefited our interpretations greatly and we are most appreciative.

The Marine Corps was particularly generous in supplying full documentation of its recruiter program from the Commandant level through local station competition programs. In particular, Lieutenant Colonel Craig Petranc, Major Steven Kendall, and Major David L. Semple were our primary liaisons. Colonel Clyde Slick reviewed the Marine Corps section of this document. We also want to acknowledge the contributions of the district commands in giving us the plans for their incentive competitions.

We also appreciate the assistance of commanders and their staffs at the many recruiting installations we visited and spoke with around the country. They increased our understanding of how incentive systems are implemented and the ways recruiters respond. They also supplied valuable documentation of local incentive programs.

We want to express our sincere appreciation for the assistance provided by Lt. Cdr. Carol Ellis and Lt. Col. Norma Tovar during their RAND fellowships and by Lt. Col. Steve Galing. We would also like to thank Jim Chiesa and Nikki Shacklett for their editing assistance and Tracy Jenkins and Jerene Kelly for their secretarial support.

ACRONYMS

ACE	New name for Navy's Production Excellence Program
AFCM	Air Force Commendation Medal
AFQT	Armed Forces Qualification Test
AH	Allied health professions
AI	Aptitude Index
AIS	Area Incentive System
APR	Accessions per Recruiter
ARMS	Automated Recruiting Management System
ASAP	Actively Seeking Another Provider
ASVAB	Armed Services Vocational Aptitude Battery
ATB	Across the Board
BMT	Basic Military Training
BSC	Biomedical Sciences Corps
CMC	Commandant of the Marine Corps
CNA	Center for Naval Analysis
CNRC	Commander, Navy Recruiting Command
CONAP	Concurrent Admissions Program
CRNA	Certified Registered Nurse Anesthetist
DEP	Delayed-entry program/pool
DTP	Delayed-training program
GA	High school graduate, I-IIIA
GED	General Equivalency Diploma
GTEP	Guaranteed Training Enlistment Program
HPSP	Health Program Scholarship Program
HQ/AFRS	Headquarters, Air Force Recruiting Service
MCD	Marine Corps District
MCRC	Marine Corps Recruiting Command
MEPS	Military Entrance Processing Stations
MSC	Medical Service Corps

NCOIC	Non-commissioned officer in charge
NPS	Non-prior service
NRCCS	Naval Recruiting Command Competition System
OPLAN	Operation Plan
OSD	Office of the Secretary of Defense
OTS	Officer Training School
PA	Physician assistant
PCS	Permanent Contract Station
PEP	Production Excellence Program
PPOD	Pivot Point Objective Delayed-Entry Program
PPOM	Pivot Point Objective Market
PT	Physical therapist
QIS	Quality Incentive System
RATE	Recruiter Advancement Through Excellence program
REIP	Recruiter Excellence Incentive Program
RMAP	Recruiter Meritorious Advancement Program
ROTC	Reserve Officer Training Corps
ROY	Recruiter of the Year
RR	Recruiting Region
RS	Recruiting Station
RSO	Recruiting Services Operations
RSS	Recruiting Sub Station
SA	High school senior, I-IIIA
TRF	Transient Recruiting Facility
TSC	Test Score Category
UMG	Upper Mental Group
USAREC	United States Army Recruiting Command

1. INTRODUCTION

Although the services have consistently met their accession targets since the beginning of the drawdown, in FY94 they began reporting increased difficulties in doing so. These reports raised concern about the services' ability to meet future accession goals, which were to rise sharply beginning in FY96. In the spring of 1994, we analyzed trends in enlisted supply and concluded that there should be an adequate supply of enlisted personnel to meet the services' goals (Asch and Orvis, 1994). Thus, to the extent that the services were reporting difficulties, we concluded that demand-side factors, such as the way recruiters were managed, might explain these difficulties.

Two key components of recruiter management are quotas and incentives. One purpose of quotas and incentives is to help motivate recruiters to work hard and efficiently to meet the services' accession targets. Another is to motivate them to allocate their effort toward enlistments that are especially valued by the services, such as high-quality candidates. To answer the question of how and whether these recruiter management tools help explain recruiting difficulties, one needs to answer two subordinate questions:

(1) How have these tools been structured? Recruiter quotas and incentives differ significantly by service and, within service, over time. These variations reflect different service cultures, recruit supply condition, and accession requirements. Unfortunately, information on quotas and incentives has not been collated in one place. Thus, answering this question is not as straightforward as it might seem.

(2) How do recruiter management tools influence recruiter behavior? Answering this question ideally requires an answer to question (1) along with recruiter-level data on recruiter characteristics and productivity. This question has not been completely answered either. Most past studies have focused on the role of recruiter goals (see, for example, Jehn and

Shughart 1996; Berner and Daula, 1993), and the few that have examined the effects of the incentive plans have focused on specific services, locations, and recruiting personnel (such as job counselors) during specific time periods (Dertouzos, 1986; Asch, 1990; Asch and Karoly, 1993; Cooke, 1987a and 1988a). While these studies suggest that the plans influence behavior, the available evidence is still insufficient to be able to draw general conclusions about which aspects of various incentives plans are the most influential, and under what circumstances

The many changes in the structure of incentive plans suggest that the services have often struggled to find the appropriate plan as recruiting conditions have changed. But determining the appropriate plan also requires answers to questions (1) and (2). Thus, the periodic redesigns that the plans undergo are done without complete information on how different aspects of the plans affect behavior.

Answering questions (1) and (2) is a large task that is beyond the scope of our project. Instead, we restrict ourselves to question (1), with a focus on incentive plans.

The report is organized by service, with one chapter devoted to each. The chapters are organized similarly, beginning with introductory material generally outlining the service's approach to recruiter incentives, to provide some orientation to the reader. There follows a section on recruiting quantity and quality goals and how they are allocated to recruiting units, e.g., stations. While our focus is on incentives, it is useful to have some information on goals or quotas because it is to facilitate fulfilling or exceeding them that incentives are established.

The bulk of each chapter is devoted to the incentive plans themselves, presented in historical order. Incentives are offered to units and individuals and are generally in the form of medals, commendations, and plaques or other mementos, though most programs also offer a limited number of promotions to the most deserving individuals. These awards have for most of the period covered been conferred on the basis of points earned for contracts written, where the point values

vary for recruits of differing aptitude or occupational specialty.
Awards may be made to units or individuals accumulating the most points
or earning a specified number of points in a period. Earning either
points or awards may be conditioned on fulfilling recruiting goals.

The main topics under each successive plan are thus the character
of the awards, the point totals or other criteria that must be met to
earn awards, and the basis for calculating points, e.g., the values of
various contract types. The order in which these are taken up varies
because each service structures its plans somewhat differently, making
it more convenient or efficient to structure the discussions somewhat
differently.

Emphasis is on national incentive plans, though some information is
provided on regional plans. Incentives are also generated locally, but
these are too numerous for treatment here. This report is further
restricted to incentives offered for recruiting enlisted personnel into
the active components. Incentives are also available for recruiting
reserve personnel and officers, but these are not addressed here except
where some acknowledgment is required to sensibly describe an enlisted
plan.

Because most chapters assume some knowledge of the Armed Forces
Qualification Test (AFQT) and delayed-entry programs (DEPs), a brief
description is offered here. The AFQT is a composite of several of the
ten components of the Armed Services Vocational Aptitude Battery, a
standard set of tests administered to all potential recruits to
determine their eligibility to enter the service and their job
qualifications. Based on their AFQT scores, recruits are placed into
classes designated by roman numerals, I (highest) to V. Class III is
divided into A and B subclasses. For a recruit to make Class I, his or
her score must be in the top 8 percent of test-takers, i.e., at the 93rd
percentile or higher. Recruits scoring at the 65th through 92nd
percentiles make Class II and those scoring in the 50th through 64th
make Class IIIA. These classes are regarded by the services as the most
desirable and incentive systems often place a premium on contracts at
that level. Class IIIB is for recruits scoring in the 31st through 49th

percentiles, Class IV for the 24th through 30th, and Class V for the bottom quarter.

Once tested, an individual may eventually sign a contract for service. In doing so, he or she typically makes a reservation for a date of entry that may be anytime from a day to months later. In the meantime, the recruit is in a delayed-entry pool. Some DEP recruits change their minds and fail to join. When the contract is written, the recruiter generally gets credit for it within the incentive system, and goals are often stated in terms of reservations placed or contracts written per month. But points may be lost when a signatory fails to show (or "ship") at the date for accession.[1] Alternatively, some incentive systems offer premiums for recruits who do eventually ship.

This recent history of recruiter incentive plans is drawn largely from archival sources and from conversations with key recruiting command staff members. In a companion report, we describe visits we made to some recruiting sites. These visits were undertaken to determine if recruiting practices and recruiter management practices have changed and what broad influences might be affecting recruiting that are not captured by explicit variables in the reestimation of our models (Asch and Orvis, 1994; Orvis et al., 1995).

---

[1]Field recruiters sometimes refer to a contract written as an "accession." In this report, "accession" refers to entry to active duty.

2. ARMY

Our review of Army incentive plans and changes to those plans begins with FY83. From November 1982 until October 1994, recruiters operated under an incentive plan called Program 300. Beginning in FY95 a new plan, Success 2000, was implemented.[1] We discuss these plans in that order, following some initial information on goals.

Every level of recruiter from field recruiters through commanders participate in the incentive programs, although the incentive structure differs by level. Army recruiters earn sequential awards by accumulating incentive points toward accomplishing individual and unit missions, and they also earn bonus points. Bonus points are awarded for contracts in specific categories and for specific command achievements. Awards are usually presented by a general officer or commanding officer at regularly scheduled ceremonies, and most are noted in the individual's record.

Additional non-point-based incentives are the Commanding General's Club and local awards programs. Each quarter the commanding general, United States Army Recruiting Command (USAREC), selects a recruiter from every recruiting battalion and publishes the individual's name in an official USAREC magazine.[2] Local awards and special ceremonies for outstanding recruiters are encouraged by USAREC. Outstanding recruiters receive certificates and special recognition.

---

[1] The Army recently eliminated Success 2000 and returned to a concept of individual missions similar to the previous program. A discussion of the new plan is beyond the scope of this report.

[2] Two key non-point incentive programs are the Secretary of the Army Recruiter Excellence Association awards. The Recruiter of the Year award began in 1984 and is awarded to an active duty and reserve army recruiter to recognize production achievement during the previous fiscal year. A plaque and certificate are presented at an official Pentagon ceremony. The Recruiter Excellence Association awards require a stated number of recruiting contracts for high school graduates or higher. The specific criteria have changed periodically to adjust for recruiting requirements since the award was initiated in 1991. Awardees receive a Chief of Staff coin, picture, certificate, and membership in the association.

GOALS

The Department of the Army establishes overall accession missions for USAREC, and USAREC then establishes contract missions and assigns them quarterly to brigades and battalions. Goals are set in terms of quantity and quality. Since the military drawdown began in 1989, Army quality objectives have been set at 95 percent with high school diplomas, around 70 percent in AFQT score categories I-IIIA , and fewer than 2 percent in the lowest test score categories. Goals are set high enough to adjust for DEP losses and other unforeseen events. For example, USAREC may set an overall recruiting battalion mission 5 percent to 15 percent higher than the number needed to meet the goal.

Brigades allocate missions down to the company level, and battalions distribute mission allocations to stations (which rank below companies).[3] These quarterly missions are translated into monthly missions using a formula developed at USAREC that accounts for historic performance and the number of days in a month. Stations assign individual monthly missions to recruiters.[4] When goals and incentive program criteria are met, awards are presented through the USAREC Incentive Awards Program.

PROGRAM 300[5]

Basis for Awards

During Program 300, a recruiter accumulating 240 points for the first time in any consecutive six-month moving window was awarded a gold star. Once that award was earned, the recruiter was awarded a second

---

[3]Informally, brigades provide substantial input to USAREC regarding battalion goals, and battalions are instrumental in determining company and individual goals. Currently there are 5 brigades, 41 battalions, and about 1,500 stations.

[4]Before FY95, individual army recruiters received specific missions and incentives designed to meet those missions. Although individual missions are not included in the incentive program from FY95 on, station commanders usually assign a specific number of monthly contracts to each recruiter.

[5]Source for Program 300 information: United States Army Recruiting Command Regulation 672-10; Recruiting Incentive Awards, various years; and United States Army Recruiting Command, *Recruiting Edge Bulletins*, September 1989 to 1st Quarter 1995.

gold star for accumulating 300 points in a subsequent consecutive six months. Further awards were obtained for additional 300-point accumulations during successive six-month moving windows, hence the program's name (see Table 2.1). Recruiters could win an award anytime during a six-month period; points in excess of those needed were applied to the next six-month window, which began the month following the award.

Table 2.1
Achievement Awards and Points: November 1982 to the Present

Award	Maximum Period[a]	Points
1st Gold Star	6 mo	240
2nd Gold Star	6 mo	300
3rd Gold Star	6 mo	300
Gold Badge	6 mo	300
1st Sapphire Star	6 mo	300
2nd Sapphire Star	6 mo	300
3rd Sapphire Star	6 mo	300
Recruiter Ring	24 mo	1,200
Glen E. Morrell Award[b]	No Time Frame	2,400

[a]October 1994; maximum period eliminated, points awarded cumulatively.
See the discussion under Success 2000 plan.
[b]October 1, 1993; added as highest award.

A Recruiter Ring, originally the top award, required 1,200 points that accrued over any consecutive 24 months. When it was discovered that a high percentage of recruiters were receiving Recruiter Rings, the Glenn E. Morrell Award was created in FY93 with a 2,400-point minimum. No time limit was placed on the new award.[6]

Point accumulation was based on contracts written toward mission (net of attrition), overproduction (contracts in excess of mission), and bonus points set by the commanding general. Contracts for high-quality

---

[6]Since 1988, all detail recruiters who earned a Recruiter Ring may be nominated by their commander for meritorious promotion from Sergeant to Staff Sergeant. Recruiters must also meet performance and conduct standards as well as specific education and training standards. About 30 promotions are awarded each year. In addition, 10 meritorious promotions from Staff Sergeant to Sergeant First Class are available annually for recruiters permanently assigned to the Army Recruiting Command.

recruits in Test Score Categories (TSC) I-IIIA were more generously
rewarded. Thus, in the fourth quarter of FY94, a contract for a high
school graduate or senior earned the recruiter 40 points if the recruit
scored in AFQT categories I, II, or IIIA (see Table 2.2). If the
recruiter had already achieved mission for recruits of that quality, the
contract was worth 70 points. Recruits scoring in category IIIB were
worth fewer points. A full table of points awarded since FY83 is in
Appendix A.

Table 2.2

Army Production and Overproduction Incentive Points
FY94

FY	FY Qtr	High School Graduate/Senior, Category I-IIIA[a]		High School Graduate/Senior, Category III B	
		Production	Over-production	Production	Over-production
94	4	40	70	20	30
94	1-3	20	60	10	30

[a]This category included currently enrolled until FY94
fourth quarter when points were restricted to high
school seniors and graduates.

Point values remained fairly consistent from FY86 through FY91. To
stimulate overproduction during those years, a 40/60 plan was in force.
This plan awarded 40 points for the first high-quality high school
graduate contract over mission, 60 points for the second overproduction,
and 20 points for each additional overproduction. After FY92, points
and point categories fluctuated more often.

How Points Accrue

Beginning in November 1982, the Program 300 incentive plan, and
subsequent revisions to the basic plan, all contained a Mission Box and
Team Concept component. Through the years, various options--Commanding
General's bonus programs, referrals programs, and other short-term
incentives--were added to or subtracted from the plan. Points for
specialized recruiters were offered in various officer programs, special
missions/special forces, and nurse programs. We do not discuss these
specialized point categories except with regard to referrals.

Mission Box

The monthly recruiting goal in specific categories assigned to units and individual recruiters is referred to as the mission box.[7] Mission box assignments include quantity and quality goals, prior-service or non-prior-service status, test score categories, and education status. Substitutions were sometimes allowed, e.g., higher-quality contracts for lower quality.

Mission box achievement merited 40 points until FY86 when the amount was changed to the 50 points currently in effect. During some years, a minimum quality requirement (e.g., one test score category I-IIIA contract) was required. Additional points could be earned for overproduction. However, a recruiter had to make mission in all categories (after subtracting any DEP losses) before overproduction points could accrue. If mission box was not achieved, individual production points were counted toward incentive awards (at half value before December 1986).

Points were calculated monthly for mission box credit and for award accumulation. For example, assume that a recruiter, in January 1992, was assigned two contracts a month--one high-quality high school graduate or senior in TSC I-IIIA and one lower-quality high school graduate or senior in TSC IIIB per month. The high-quality graduate was worth 20 production points or 50 overproduction points, and the lower-quality recruit was worth 10 production points and 20 overproduction points. The recruiter was successful and wrote both assigned contracts and two additional lower-quality contracts. Points for January were awarded as follows:

Mission box	50
Overproduction points	40
Total points applied to award accumulation	90

---

[7]Individuals were assigned specific geographic recruiting areas along with goals. They recruited only in their zone and had to refer outside potential recruits to the appropriate recruiter.

This recruiter received 40 additional points toward an award because mission box was achieved. If this recruiter failed to make monthly mission and wrote only, for example, three low-quality contracts, then the point award would be 10 points for each contract, or 30 points applied toward point accumulation. If an individual's combined point total for all the contracts was higher when not counting mission box, then the higher point total was awarded. When more points than were necessary for an award were achieved, any points over mission box were carried forward.

Recruiting units achieved mission box by fulfilling both regular army and reserve army quantity and quality goal assignments (unless the unit was a single mission unit recruiting only one type of recruit). Unit accomplishment was sometimes required before individual awards could be presented.[8]

Mission box was not calculated solely on a monthly basis. In 1993 and 1994, an additional 25 points were awarded to individuals if they achieved quarterly mission box.[9] In all other years, quarterly mission box was awarded points by the commanding general.

Team Concept Points

The team concept program was developed to allow recruiting personnel not achieving mission box to receive points when the total mission box assigned to their unit was achieved. Team concept criteria changed in December 1985 so that points could be awarded to a recruiter even if his or her unit did not make mission box, as long as it achieved the total quantity or quality mission assigned when a higher-level command achieved mission box. Recruiting brigade and USAREC personnel did not receive points, but mission box achieved at those levels affected lower-level awards.

---

[8]Unit commanders competed for awards based on unit accomplishment using a variety of formulas depending on the unit level. Recruiting station commanders with an assigned individual mission could compete using unit accomplishment or their individual point total.

[9]The monthly mission box award increased the likelihood that high or overachievers would space contracts over the three months to receive both monthly and quarterly mission box points.

The maximum points available through team concept was 40 until FY86, then 50. Until FY89, overproduction, bonus, and referral points were not counted when team concept was applied. Since FY89, bonus points and referral points (until they were eliminated in FY94) were allowed, but overproduction points were not permitted. From May 1989 through FY94, team concept points could be awarded if the regular army mission was achieved at the lower level and the reserve mission at the higher level, or vice-versa.

Commanding General's Bonus Points

The Commanding General of the Army Recruiting Command periodically awarded bonus points for various reasons such as meeting specific recruiting needs or rewarding ongoing targeted categories. The bonus categories and point levels were announced monthly by message. High-quality graduates, accepted delayed-entry and delayed-training program (DTP) memberships, and quarterly mission box accomplishments were consistently rewarded. Special awards for particular categories and courtesy ship of DEP and DTP accessions were added and removed periodically.[10] At any one time there were up to 9 categories ranging from 5 to 50 points.

Referral Points

From 1982 through 1993, referrals by enlisted recruiters to specialty recruiters for particular programs or categories such as chaplain, military academy, Army National Guard, etc., were rewarded with 10 points when enlistment contracts were written.[11] Referrals to the Army Nurse Corps was rewarded with 20 points when the applicant was accepted. Point schemes for Reserve Officer Training Corps (ROTC) and Warrant Officer referrals were added in FY90. The referral program was discontinued because audits revealed that recruiters were using

---

[10]Courtesy ship refers to recruits who sign a contract at one recruiting station but report to duty at another recruiting station. Since a contract must be written and a recruit must report to duty if points are to accumulate permanently, the points awarded may be divided between the two responsible recruiters.

[11]Army Nurse Corps recruiters also received 10 points when they sent referrals to regular army recruiters.

referrals to receive awards without achieving their mission, thereby negating the production program.

SUCCESS 2000[12]

Rationale and Basis for Awards

In FY95, USAREC changed the way individual recruiters and recruiting units are assigned production goals, incentive programs are designed, and recruiting accomplishment is rewarded. The new program, Success 2000, retains many concepts from previous years such as mission box, bonus points, team concept, and incentive awards. However, in an effort to emphasize teamwork, to focus leaders' and commanders' efforts on meeting recruiting goals, and to increase high-quality enlistments, recruiting station allocations and awards categories are now simplified. A key feature of this new program is a change from focusing on individual achievement to focusing on team effort.

Success 2000 was developed primarily because the Army was meeting its annual accession mission, but units and individuals were failing to achieve their contract mission. For example, in any given month of FY92, the most successful Recruiting Command year, 75 percent of battalions did not meet their mission. In recent years, up to 80 percent of battalions did not meet their monthly mission.[13] Not meeting command goals results in low morale and disciplinary actions, producing a win/lose situation. The new team mission concept allows the entire team to win by accounting for recruiting inconsistencies such as recruiters who periodically are unable to achieve their individual contract mission.

The new program is designed to simplify attaining mission by reducing the number of mission box categories and to encourage teamwork. Under this plan, recruiters work as a team to find the recruits necessary to meet the station mission. More experienced recruiters are encouraged to help less experienced recruiters. In addition, the

---

[12]Source: *Success 2000*, United States Army Recruiting Headquarters Memorandum, August 29, 1994, and September 21, 1994.

[13]Source: *Success 2000 Memorandum*, Information Paper, July 5, 1994.

simpler categories reduce the need for recruiters to focus their attention on different types of recruits each month (depending on the mission assigned for that month). Instead, they can build up a market and continue their activities as long as the market is fruitful. Recruiters continue to receive individual points and bonus points that are counted toward awards, but they do not receive mission box points unless the station fulfills its regular and reserve army mission. In addition, higher command-level success is determined by the percentage of successful stations as well as the percentage of successful recruiters. To meet their mission, the commands above recruiting station are expected to concentrate on assisting less successful stations.

An additional feature of the new program is an expansion of the recruiting station commander's authority, autonomy, and flexibility. As mentioned above, it used to be that each recruiter was assigned a particular geographic area. Now the entire recruiting area is treated as one market, and all recruiters work the entire market. The recruiting station commander can focus on productive marketing areas and direct recruiters according to their strengths and abilities rather than creating boundaries. High schools continue to be assigned to specific recruiters.

Success 2000 retains the existing Incentive Awards point and award structure but removes time limits and sliding windows. Points are calculated monthly and are cumulative and awards are issued as the required points are accrued. Unit mission box and individual production points are counted toward awards. With Success 2000's broad emphasis on teamwork, the separate team concept program was eliminated.

How Points Accrue

As illustrated in Table 2.3, individual production points include points in specified categories for enlisted contracts written, bonus points, accession points when a recruit reports to duty, and mission box if the recruiting station achieves mission box. Recruiting unit points are calculated to determine if the team makes mission by adding production recruiter points and bonus points and then dividing by the number of production recruiters assigned to the unit.[14] Recruiting units do not get mission box points. Individual points are calculated as part of the station mission and to determine individual awards.

Table 2.3

Success 2000 Regular Army Mission Box and Incentive Awards Points[a]

Category	Points
Mission Box	50
High school graduate I-IIIA (GA)	30
High school senior I-IIIA (SA)	20
Other (prior service, other high school and non-high school graduate, no mental category)	10
Commanding General's Bonus	
Quarterly recruiting station mission box	40
Band contracts	10
Concurrent Admissions Program (CONAP)[b]	5
Accessions	20
Recruiting station leader[c]	
Each contract written over mission box	20

[a]Points and bonus points for specific officer, army reserve, and nurse contracts are also awarded in Success 2000 to individual recruiters who specialize in writing contracts in these categories.

[b]CONAP encourages college-capable persons to postpone college to enlist in the Army.

[c]On-production station commander (writing contracts) choosing not to compete as an individual.

Success 2000 stresses accessions and awards 20 points for each enlistee reporting for duty. (This appears to be an effort to reduce DEP losses.) In the past, accessions were rewarded only periodically such as the Commanding General's Bonus during Operation Desert Shield/Storm.

---

[14]Under certain conditions, the number of assigned recruiters may be adjusted to account for absences during a full month that prevent a recruiter from producing contracts. These conditions include: convalescent leave, maternity leave, emergency leave, removed from station, and some school leave.

Mission Box

Success 2000 changes mission box by reducing the box to three categories from as many as 20 previously, eliminating overproduction points for recruiters, and removing individual mission boxes. Individual recruiting station commanders usually assign a monthly goal to each recruiter, but this goal is no longer applied toward an individual mission box. Each station awards 50 mission box points to all recruiters when the combined regular army and reserve army station mission (goal) is achieved. Mission box points are added to all production points the individual recruiter achieves in each of the categories in Table 2.3. The entire recruiting station is focused on accomplishing a combined regular and reserve army mission box. Mission box points are no longer awarded above station level. Higher-level units, however, continue to receive goals in mission box categories.

Points are applied toward achievement awards as described previously. In Success 2000, high-quality recruits are the focus, and those contracts are most highly rewarded. Individual monthly points for a hypothetical recruiter in a station that achieves mission box would be calculated as follows:

Category	Points
Mission box	50
Individual production points	
1- GA	30
1- Other	10
1-Accession	20
Total bonus points	0
Total points awarded	110

Using this same recruiter, if the station did not achieve mission box, then 60 points would be counted toward the recruiter's incentive award accumulation.

Contracts for high school graduates in TSC I-IIIA are the only allowable substitution for the 10 and 20 point mission box categories. That means if a station does not meet its mission for high school seniors in TSC I-IIIA or other, a contract for a high school graduate in TSC I-IIIA can substitute. Unlike the past, no further points are added for a substitution.

In contrast to previous years, recruiters receive no additional points for overproduction in Success 2000. While overproduction in categories is necessary to accomplish overall goals, eliminating the stress on recruiter overproduction allows leaders and commanders to focus on improving unsuccessful units. However, leaders and commanders do encourage overproduction where appropriate, and they receive points for each contract written over mission.[15]

Commanding General's Bonus Points

Commanding General's Bonus point categories and awards continue to be announced quarterly. The FY95 Success 2000 Commanding General's Bonus is awarded in three categories: (1) Quarterly mission box was increased from a high of 15 points to 40 points, (2) specified band (and two specialized medical categories) contracts receive 10 points, and (3) the CONAP receives 5 points after each contract is accepted.[16] These bonuses spotlight specific needs and encourage team effort.

---

[15]On-production station commanders, who are commanders that write individual contracts, can choose to compete as individuals and earn points, or they can compete as recruiting station leaders. Recruiting station leaders include limited production commanders of stations with 5 or more recruiters and on-production commanders choosing to compete in this category. Leaders are awarded mission box points for successful station accomplishment and 20 recruiting station leader points for each contract over mission box.

[16]CONAP is a program to encourage college-capable men and women who are postponing college for financial or other reasons to enlist in the army. The army helps arrange college enrollment in participating schools, and helps recruits obtain credit in the selected school for college-required courses taken during their tour of duty. The enrollment slot is held until military service is completed.

3. NAVY

Our review of Navy recruiter incentive plans covers the last 17 years. During that period, two types of systems have usually operated concurrently. One type has rewarded recruiter achievement with promotions or credits toward promotion, and the other with command recognition, trips, plaques, commendations, and gifts. Plans have changed during the period covered, and the chapter is divided into sections marked off by the years of greatest change.

The Navy recruiting operation is managed through several command levels. The Commander, Navy Recruiting Command, supervises recruiting and sets policy at the national level. The nation is divided into geographic areas that have primary responsibility for implementing national policy and overseeing regional activities. Areas are divided into districts that manage day-to-day operations and set local policies. Under the districts are recruiting zones and stations. At the present time there are 4 areas, 31 districts (4-5 zones per district), and a variable number of stations per zone. This structure has changed over time. Since 1979, the number of areas has decreased from 8 to 4, and the number of districts has decreased from 41 to 31. Achievement has been rewarded at all levels of the recruiting command structure.

GOALS

National recruiting efforts begin at the Department of the Navy Headquarters, where overall annual manpower requirements are decided. The Navy Recruiting Command determines recruiting goals and priorities for the areas and makes recommendations for district goals. Currently, the Research and Analysis Division of the Recruiting Command's Plans and Policies Department has primary responsibility for determining how many new contracts each area and its associated districts must write to meet annual accession requirements.[1]

In addition, areas receive targets for the proportion of recruits required to be high-school graduates and in AFQT categories I, II, or

---

[1]New contracts refer to first-time enlistments.

IIIA.[2] In the years between FY84 and FY95, the proportion of non-prior-service recruits required to meet these criteria ranged from 57.5 percent to 65 percent. Currently, 95 percent of new recruits must hold high school diplomas. Quality goals are set for overall enlistments as well as for blacks, Hispanics, and Asians and Pacific Islanders. Policies are also established annually for special programs such as the Navy College Fund, for recruiting in Puerto Rico, and for recruits in specialized or technical fields of knowledge.[3]

The Research and Analysis Division calculates shares of the goals with analytical methods that include regression analysis.[4] The Division also calculates how many recruits must report to duty each month to assure that training classes are full and force size is maintained. After the shares are determined, the Research and Analysis Division converts the shares into monthly numbers and distributes them to the areas. The area commander, using the Division's district recommendations as a guide, distributes goals to the districts and reports the final allocation distribution. The last step in this process is monitoring by the Research and Analysis Division based on daily computerized enlistment data and monthly reports from the areas.[5]

Before FY90, the individual recruiter received a specific goal to write a given number of contracts. Now there are no formal individual goals, but recruiters are informally aware of their expected contribution to the overall unit goal. That is, some recruiter supervisors require recruiters to write at least one contract a month as a minimum standard.

---

[2]The Navy does not recognize Alternate Credential Holders (e.g., General Equivalency Diploma (GED)), or other special high school graduation programs as equivalent to a high school diploma.

[3]Active Duty Enlisted Recruiting Goals and Policies, Navy Recruiting Command, Notice 1133, Annual Instruction.

[4]The equation includes variables such as civilian population and wages, number of recruiters, advertising funds, youth attitudes about military service, and dummies for recruit quality level and seasonal variations. In addition, the final goals are adjusted for past performance, experience level of recruiters, and recruiter effort required to meet the goal.

[5]The goal allocation process described in this section was followed throughout the entire study period, although the responsible branches changed.

INCENTIVE PLANS, FY79 TO FY90

The primary incentive system during this period was the Freeman Plan, a national system created to reward individual recruiter productivity with promotion awards or points, extension of duty, medals, and commendations. The Navy Recruiting Command Competition System provided incentives for goal attainment and presented command recognition or other awards. A Gold and Silver Wreath incentive system was also offered during this time. These programs are described below.

Freeman Plan[6]

The Navy's Recruiter Productivity and Personnel Management System, commonly known as the Freeman Plan, was in force from 1979 through FY88. The plan made requirements for, and offered incentives to, all production recruiters, i.e., those who were actively enlisting recruits.

Requirements. The Freeman Plan required meeting a minimum average quota of two gross new contracts over a two-month period.[7] When a recruiter did not maintain the new contract average over any four-month period and was not able to comply with monthly warnings and or benefit from assistance to improve, a nomination for transfer to a different duty assignment was necessary. New recruiters did not have to meet this requirement until the fifth and sixth months on duty.

Point System. Points in the Freeman Plan were accumulated over a twelve-month production period (with up to an additional three quarters of a month for excused time), but were calculated monthly and reported monthly. In contrast to the bi-monthly contract requirement, incentive point accumulation was reported in net terms, accounting for attrition. Incentive points were calculated each month on a computer reservation system.[8] This system was programmed to produce net contract reports by deducting reservation cancellations and attritions from contracts written. Accessions, that is, recruits reporting for duty, were

---

[6]Source: *Recruiter Productivity and Personnel Management System "The Freeman Plan,"* Chapter 8, Navy Recruiting Command; Asch (1990).

[7]Gross contracts are all contracts written without deductions for attrition.

[8]When a contract was written and job classification determined, a space was reserved until the recruit reported for duty.

credited to the original reservation month, while attritions were debited in the month they occurred, resulting in the possibility of lost points up to one year after a contract is signed.

The Freeman Plan point system rewarded contracts as shown in Table 3.1. Although the point award amounts clearly favored those who enlisted recruits with high test scores and high school diplomas, it was possible for an aggressive recruiter to earn sufficient award points by writing only lower-quality contracts. When an enlisted recruiter encountered a potential officer recruit and provided a referral, he or she could also receive Freeman Plan points under certain conditions.[9]

Table 3.1

Freeman Plan Point Values

AFQT Category	High School Graduates	Non-High School Graduates
I	116	100
II	107	90
IIIA	100	85
IIIB	90	65
IV	70	N/A

Rewards. Table 3.2 shows the Freeman Plan's recruiter rewards and their required 12-month average points. At the end of 12 months "on production," the recruiter was granted an award if his or her annual average of monthly points was at least 300. If the recruiter won an award, a new 12-month production cycle began. If the annual average was under 300 per month, points continued to be calculated in a moving 12-month average until 300 points were achieved. Awards were distributed at the discretion of the district commander and could be denied if other attributes of the individual's performance, such as conduct or personal appearance, were not satisfactory.

---

[9]130 points were awarded when a referred officer candidate for the nuclear propulsion program entered Officer Candidate School. 100 points were awarded when a referred nuclear program collegiate candidate started receiving Navy pay. When a referral entered the officer program from the DEP, the original recruiter's entitlement to point retention was determined for each case individually by Navy Recruiting Command.

Table 3.2

**Recruiter Rewards and Promotion Points, and Required
12-Month-Average Freeman Plan Points**

Reward	Average Points Required
1. Meritorious advancement	525
2. Voluntary extension	400
3. Navy Achievement Medal (2 promotion points)[a]	350
4. Certificate of Commendation (1 promotion point)[b]	300

[a]A Navy Commendation Medal (worth 3 promotion points) replaces a third consecutive Navy Achievement Medal.

[b]A Navy Achievement Medal replaces a third consecutive Certificate of Commendation.

Meritorious promotion to a higher paygrade was the highest award presented and required 525 points averaged over 12 months. Only recruiters meeting both the point requirement and the usual Navy promotion requirements, i.e., specified active time in service, could be nominated for meritorious advancement. Some recruiters at higher paygrade levels (E7 and E8) who met these requirements also received a Navy Achievement Medal, and an offer to extend their tour of duty one year (if they were at 8 to 10 months of projected rotation date).

Recruiters with 400 average monthly points were given the same duty extension offer. A recruiter was eligible to earn this award any number of times. This award was valued by recruiters because it extended shore duty for those in occupations requiring lengthy sea duty. The extended assignment to recruiting service also increased opportunities for recruiters to obtain promotions in the incentive program.

The last two awards--the Navy Achievement Medal, awarded for 350 average monthly points, and the Certificate of Commendation, awarded for 300 average monthly points--were sources of promotion points. Promotion points were added to national proficiency exam points (required of all promotion applicants) to increase promotion opportunities for paygrades E4 through E6. For higher-paygrade promotions, the points were considered by national selection boards along with other annual criteria. Promotions were not guaranteed, but occurred when positions were available. The Navy Achievement Medal was worth two promotion points and the Certificate of

Commendation was worth one promotion point. After two consecutive Navy Achievement Medals, a Navy Commendation Medal worth three promotion points was awarded. After two consecutive Certificates of Commendation, a Navy Achievement Medal was awarded. By awarding additional points for sustained accomplishment, the Freeman Plan motivated lower-scoring recruiters during their entire three-year tour of duty.

Eventually the plan was discontinued for two reasons. First, there was a concern that recruiters used the system in ways that adversely affected achieving quantity and quality goals. For example, some recruiters chose to submit contracts at a time favorable for assuring an award rather than in compliance with overall monthly Navy enlistment requirements; or, to achieve sufficient points for a reward, some recruiters solicited a large quantity of easier to acquire low-quality recruits, rather than fewer, but more difficult to obtain high-quality enlistments. Second, there were concerns about inequities in the system that could not be adjusted to ensure that every recruiter had an equal chance to earn Freeman Plan awards regardless of differences in recruit markets or recruiting management.[10]

Annual Awards[11]

The Competition System. The Annual Awards program rewards top-performing area and district commands and individuals in various categories. Until FY90, these awards were based on the Navy Recruiting Command Competition System. In this system, the award was determined by a point system and provided national and area recognition. Point allocations (different from Freeman Plan points) for each enlistment category were decided annually by the Commander, Navy Recruiting Command.[12] Generally, there were five to seven achievement categories (depending on the year), rewarding goal attainment in such categories as

---

[10]Source: Conversations with various members of the Navy Recruiting Command staff.

[11]Source: Navy Recruiting Command Instructions 1650.8G to 1650.8J, *Navy Recruiting Command Competition System*, FY87 to FY90.

[12]The formulas for calculating annual points in each category were revised each year to reflect the value of contract types relative to overall recruiting goals. Some categories rewarded goal attainment and overproduction, while others only rewarded overproduction. (FY89 formulas are reprinted in Appendix B as an example of the format and method used.)

total new contracts written, nuclear field contracts written, non-prior-service accessions, black upper-mental-group (AFQT I-IIIA) accessions, and Hispanic upper-mental-group accessions. The areas and districts were ranked by their point totals.

Awards. Units were nominated by area commanders for such awards as District of the Year and Most Improved District. The physical award for these categories was a trophy signifying national recognition. These awards were presented either at a national conference or by a national officer at a regional meeting. Recruiting Pennant ("R" pennant) awards were presented to districts that were the top districts in their areas.

Individuals were nominated by their commanders for national or area awards. The awards included a promotion opportunity for the Recruiter of the Year (ROY), medals, commendations, letters, attendance at annual ROY Week activities, trophies, file notes, and membership in select groups. Winners included recruiting supervisors, field recruiters, and support and civilian personnel.

Gold and Silver Wreath Program

The Gold and Silver Wreath Program rewarded recruiting goal achievement over short time periods, e.g., a few months. A recruit quality component was not included in the wreath program. Gold wreaths were awarded to production personnel, and silver wreaths to support personnel. The wreaths were made of metal and surrounded the Recruiter Badge. To receive a gold wreath, recruiters were required to write 14 contracts in three consecutive months or less, and they also had to pass subjective performance and personal evaluations. A recruiter achieving the same goal in the next consecutive three months could win additional awards, usually a star. Supervisors received gold wreaths if their unit achieved quarterly recruiting goals. Support personnel received silver wreaths for exemplary service over at least six consecutive months.[13]

---

[13]Lerro et al. (1989), and conversations with recruiting staff provided information for this paragraph.

Other Programs

In addition to the formal national programs, areas and districts developed awards to account for unique features in their area, and to reward their own successful recruiters. These programs were usually short-term competitions, and bonus point opportunities. The winners were awarded certificates, plaques, or trophies.

INCENTIVE PLANS, FY90 TO FY94

To improve incentives for enlisting enough high-quality recruits to meet national Navy goals, a new overall plan to reward recruiting team and individual accomplishment with promotion opportunities was introduced for FY90 and remained in force through the first quarter of FY94. The main feature of this new plan was an emphasis on rewarding team effort in meeting recruiting goals and Navy performance standards. A team could be as large as an area or as small as a recruiting station. Both recruiter promotions and awards were retained as incentives. As in the past, local incentive programs were also encouraged.

The new plan included two programs--the Recruiter Meritorious Advancement Program (RMAP) and the Recruiter Advancement Through Excellence (RATE) program. Both programs provided recruiter promotion opportunities, but RMAP was based on individual recruiter goal attainment, and RATE was based on team production beyond goal attainment, i.e., overproduction. Promotion nominations were decided by special recruiting awards boards at the district level, and selections were made at the national level. Both RATE and RMAP were modified and combined in March 1993 and renamed the Recruiter Excellence Incentive Program (REIP). REIP is the promotion system currently in effect.

Meanwhile, the Annual Awards program continued. For the first half of FY90, it was based on a revised version of the Competition System described above. Competition was changed from a contest among all areas and districts at the national level to an area-specific competition for district awards. Each area nominated its best district for selection in the Annual Awards program. This change was instituted to allow areas to create their own enlistment contract incentives and categories. The revisions were designed to provide more flexibility to area commanders, but the FY90 plan did not work well because it was deemed too cumbersome, and the Competition System was terminated.

The Annual Awards program, previously associated with the Competition System, was retained. It was based on a new competition within areas and their districts. The way incentive points were calculated was revised. To help units uniformly rank recruiter team production and levels of emphasis, a Quality Incentive System (QIS) was created that assigned point values for specific recruiting categories. Points were reported only for areas, districts, zones, and stations.

Overproduction/Promotion Incentive Programs[14]

Recruiter Meritorious Advancement Program (RMAP). This program was in effect from 10/1/89 to 4/28/93 and was established to provide special recognition for superior performance by individual production recruiters. Recruiters in paygrade levels E5 and E6 were eligible to compete. Under the RMAP, 57 E6 promotions were allocated each year. Headquarters distributed 47 to the districts (2 each to the six largest districts, and 1 each to the others). The other ten promotions were set aside until the end of the year to be given to districts with unusually large numbers of outstanding recruiters. There were 14 promotions to E7 available annually. District commanders submitted narrative nomination letters to the Commander, Navy Recruiting Command, for each promotion candidate.

To qualify for an E6 or E7 promotion nomination, a recruiter needed to demonstrate outstanding personal and professional qualities as well as superior recruiting success. The commander was encouraged to stress team spirit and qualities as a team player when nominating a candidate. Advancing to E6 also required 12 months minimum recruiting duty immediately before advancement and three years of service as an E5. . Those advancing to E7 required 18 months minimum recruiting duty immediately before advancement and three years of service as an E6. All nominees also met testing, physical, and moral requirements before

---

[14]Source: Various versions of Navy Recruiting Command Instruction 1430.1, 1430.1A, and 1430.1A Change 1 and 2.

advancement. Final decisions on advancements were issued by the
Commander, Navy Recruiting Command.

   Recruiter Advancement Through Excellence (RATE). This program was
created to offer promotion opportunities in addition to RMAP. RATE
rewarded districts that overproduced, and was intended to stimulate
districts to work as teams. The program was open to all E4 through E7
personnel including classifiers (job counselors) who met the usual Navy
promotion requirements in addition to the requirement of contributing to
overall group performance.[15] Promotions to E5 and E6 were made directly
by the district commander, while those to E7 and E8 were selected from
nominations to a national command selection board.[16]

   Promotion allocations were assigned to districts by the Commander,
Navy Recruiting Command. Up to 90 E7 and 12 E8 promotions could be
awarded annually across districts. The percentage of E5 and E6
nominations available to each district was determined using a table in
the RATE instruction. Each district was allowed to nominate 1 percent
of its senior personnel for every 1 percent of production over its
annual New Contract Objective goals up to 106 percent (see Appendix C
for precise formulas).[17] Overproduction was a quantity and quality
measure incorporating both the percentage of new contract goal achieved
and the percentage of high-quality goal achieved. Those nominated for
E7 and E8 but not selected were given Letters of Commendation from the
Chief of Naval Personnel to improve their consideration for regular
promotions.

   When a district's new contract production did not meet
overproduction criteria, promotions could still be awarded within zones
demonstrating extraordinary production. Zone formulas for promotion
availability were similar to the district formulas, but the percentage
of recruiters eligible at the zone level was smaller than at the
district level. (See Appendix C for zone formulas.)

---

   [15]Classifiers competed under the same incentive structure as
recruiters.
   [16]Some districts convened district boards to select nominees at all
levels, but this was not required.
   [17]Districts also received annual reports of the number of eligible
recruiters from Recruiting Command.

In July 1991, the RATE program was amended. To improve advancement selection fairness, district selection boards were created to consider all aspects of a recruiter's performance, not just contracts written. Criteria for selecting district board members were clarified, a timely submission date was established, E5 and E6 rules were extensively revised, and advancements were limited to either one RATE or one RMAP award per recruiter, even if he or she were nominated in both categories. In April 1992, a quality variable was added to the district-level formula to encourage recruiters to enlist high-quality recruits. The zone-level formula was also revised to provide greater opportunity for zone-level promotions.

Recruiter Excellence Incentive Program (REIP). This program was implemented on April 28, 1993. It replaces and combines elements of the previous RATE and RMAP programs to provide promotion opportunities for outstanding recruiters (see Table 3.3). All recruiting personnel in paygrades E4 to E6, except career recruiters, are eligible for promotion nomination in this program.

Table 3.3
RMAP, RATE, and REIP Overproduction/Promotion Incentive Programs

	RMAP	RATE	REIP
Effective dates	10/1/89-4/28/93	10/1/89-4/28/93	4/28/93 to present
Reward	Promotions to E6 and E7	Promotions to E5-E8	Promotions to E5-E7
Number available	57 E6 and 14 E7 promotions	E5 and E6 by formula, 90 E7 and 12 E8 promotions	7% avg. FY manning by formula, 1/50/ district
Requirements	Superior performance	Quantity and quality over-production	Quantity and quality overproduction and superior performance
Eligible	E6, 12 months and E7, 18 months on board	E4-E7 including classifiers	E4-E6, 15 months on board

Meritorious Promotions. Under REIP, individuals are rewarded for superior performance in contributing to mission performance at the district level. To be eligible, recruiters must take the Navy promotion exam, serve the prescribed time as a recruiter, and may not have been meritoriously advanced to their present paygrade. Promotions are awarded at the rate of one for each fifty district enlisted personnel (or fraction thereof) each fiscal year.

Production Promotions. These are rewards to outstanding recruiters in overproducing districts. Production promotions are authorized only in years when the entire Navy achieves its accession and quality goals. To qualify, a district must also achieve its goals. When advancements are awarded, a national total of one per fifty (or fraction thereof) average national fiscal year recruiting staff will be eligible. Districts receive advancement allocations according to formulas similar to the previous RATE formulas. These calculations are based on the degree to which the district exceeds its fiscal year quantity and quality goals. The formulas for Production Promotions are calculated monthly at the district level to track the number of eligible achievers in a district. On the last day of the fiscal year, the district performs a final promotion calculation using a final annual national eligibility rate and end-of-FY district calculations. (See Appendix D for formulas.)

Nationally, the limit for REIP promotions (meritorious and production) is 7 percent of average enlisted fiscal year manning (the long standing Navy-wide standard). To spur lagging enlistments in 1989, advancements were increased to 9 percent, but this limit could not be sustained, and an official 7 percent cap was incorporated in Commander, Navy Recruiting Command, Instructions.

Some district commanders use a district or area point system to rank individual performance when selecting nominees for promotion, but there is no formal point requirement. In FY93, REIP promotion nominations required twelve continuous months on board as a recruiter, but in FY94 the minimum changed to fifteen months.

Annual Awards

The Quality Incentive System. QIS was created to emphasize critical recruiting categories and quality levels and provide incentive to write contracts in them. QIS encouraged competition among recruiting teams for points. Points were recorded and calculated at the district level and were used as a measure for nominations to the Annual Awards program. Districts were required to use QIS points as the only measure for zone and station awards in this competition system. Since individuals were not assigned goals as under the Freeman Plan, individual points were not officially reported, but they were calculated and used to track recruiter performance. Recruiters could not be rewarded or disciplined based solely on their individual point accumulation. However, the rankings informally helped to determine promotion nominations. The individual points were not tracked at the national level, although they were available to awards boards at that level on request.

QIS competition points were developed annually from FY90 through FY94 by the Research and Analysis Division, Plans and Policy Department, Commander, Navy Recruiting Command. With the input and approval of the Commander, the Research and Analysis Division set point values for achieving or exceeding monthly enlistment contract goals in specific enlistment categories. If recruiting requirements changed during the year, points were adjusted appropriately. QIS was abolished in February 1994 when all forms of point competition at the national level were terminated. The QIS point categories and their annual assigned point values from FY90 through FY94 are shown in Table 3.4.

The goal categories counting toward the QIS score varied with recruiting level. Stations and zones calculated points for Basic Contracts (new contract goal achieved), Workforce (defined as ready to report for duty immediately between May and October), "A" Cell (recruits in highest quality level), black and Hispanic upper mental groups, and recruits qualified and accepted into the Nuclear Field Program. Districts and areas were judged on the categories described above with the addition of Pivot Point Objective Delayed Entry Program (PPOD, a system to control DEP size), Pivot Point Objective Market (PPOM, a system to control the mix of contracts written for high school students and non-high school graduate recruits), admiral's emphasis, and accessions (shipping attainment).

Table 3.4

Quality Incentive System (QIS) Weights: FY 90 To February 1994

Category	FY90	FY91	FY92	Feb FY92	FY93	Apr FY93	May FY93	FY94
Basic contract	1	3	3	3	3	3	3	2
Male	1							
Female	0.5				2	2		
Black upper mental group	0.5	1	1.5	1.5	1.5	1.5	1.5	1
Hispanic upper mental group	0.5	1	1.5	1.5				
Nuclear field	0.5	1	1	1	1			
Workforce	0.75							4
Navy veteran	1							
A-cell (mental category A)		5	6	6				
Male workforce		5		3				
Upper mental group					6	6	6	4
PPOD		1						1
PPOM		1			1	1	1	1
Accession		1			1	1	1	1
Admiral's emphasis		1			1	1	1	1
Overall QIS		3			3	3	3	3

SOURCE: Commander, Navy Recruiting Command, Research Studies Branch of the Research Division, Lieutenant Briggs, November 1994.

The basic QIS calculation involved multiplying the incentive points in Table 3.4 by the contracts in each goal category, summing the products, and then dividing by the product sum representing attainment of all goals. An overall QIS score of "1" (or larger) represents goal attained or overproduction, on average, across all categories.

Table 3.5 illustrates the way a district QIS score was determined and points were awarded in FY91 using points shown in Table 3.4. Based on Table 3.5, then,

$$QIS = 734/730 = 1.00548$$

If PPOD, PPOM, and accessions all were attained (100 percent), the unit would have received 1 point each for a total of 3 points that would have been added to three times the QIS total, i.e.:

Table 3.5

Illustrative QIS Point Calculation

	Points per Contract	Contract Goal	Total Point Goal	Contracts Obtained	Total Points Obtained
Basic contracts	3	100	300	100	300
"A" Cell	5	80	400	81	405
Hispanic upper mental group	1	10	10	9	9
Black upper mental group	1	10	10	10	10
Nuclear field	1	10	10	10	10
Total			730		734

1.00548 x 3 overall QIS points = 3.016438

3.016438 + 3 (PPOD, PPOM, accessions) = 6.016438

Total QIS points submitted for QIS competition = 6.016438.

Awards. Awards for individuals and units are based on nomination submissions from areas and districts to the Commander, Navy Recruiting Command. Submissions for units considered QIS points along with other criteria.

Unit awards in FY94 included outstanding districts and stations in twelve different categories such as Recruiting District of the Year; Large, Small, and Medium Stations of the Year; and Most Improved District. Rewards ranged from trophies to attendance at the annual national ROY Week festivities.[18]

Individual awards in FY94 were given in twenty recruiter categories (including job counselors) such as Best Overall, Area Best, and District Best, Zone Best and Support Best of the Year. Rewards in these categories included Meritorious Promotion, Navy Commendation Medals, Navy Achievement Medals, Letters of Commendation, Trophies, and ROY Week attendance. Appendix E contains tables of the FY94 unit and individual categories and awards.

---

[18]Source: *Navy Recruiting Command Individual and Unit Annual Incentive Awards,* Navy Recruiting Command Instruction 1650.16D, March 15, 1994.

Gold Wreath

The Gold Wreath program continued to provide recognition to individual production recruiters and to support and civilian personnel satisfying general billet requirements for conduct and performance as well as specific district production goals. For example, production recruiters are eligible for a wreath when they write eight net contracts in three consecutive months and also meet all other district requirements.[19] Support personnel now also receive gold wreaths rather than silver, while civilians receive a miniature wreath. Recruiters can win as many as 50 awards in this program. A schedule of awards issued in a designated order on a periodic schedule specifies the initial Gold Wreath followed by silver and gold stars, and Letters of Commendation from increasingly higher authority. Production personnel can begin receiving awards immediately after assignment to production. Support personnel must satisfy six months of excellent performance for eligibility.

INCENTIVE PLANS, FY94 TO THE PRESENT

The current Navy incentive programs are the REIP, the Individual and Unit Annual Awards Program, and the Gold Wreath Program, as described above. However, it is no longer required that nominations for Annual Awards to units be based on QIS. Since the second half of FY94, areas and districts create their own plans to provide incentives for units and individuals to write the contracts necessary to achieve national goals. Area and district awards to achieve local goals continue.

To replace QIS, all four areas were required to submit incentive plans to the Commander, Navy Recruiting Command, in March 1994. Currently, Area Eight, encompassing the West Coast and Rocky Mountains, continues to operate an area plan, while the other areas allow districts to develop their own plans, or not, as the district commander determines is appropriate for that district. The following are examples of area plans submitted in 1994.

_____

[19]The revised Gold Wreath program is described in Navy Recruiting Command Instruction 1650.4K, change order 2, effective 3/28/94.

- Area One, in the Northeast, presented awards to a monthly zone supervisor, and "Heavy Hitter" and "Captain's Cup" awards to all who performed within prescribed limits. A quarterly best zone and station were selected by a board. As short-term needs arose, specific incentives were offered. Most districts in Area One retained a basic QIS format but added categories or changed point awards to suit their requirements. Some districts also modified the way winners were chosen in the competition system.

- Area Three provided a Master Manager Award (Letter of Commendation and personalized wall clock) for outstanding performance among Recruiters in Charge of a three-person or larger station. The award was based on goal attainment and other qualifications. Zone and zone supervisor of the quarter were rewarded for attaining the highest total percentage of goals according to the following formula: (% new contract goal attained + % total upper mental group goal attained + %workforce - attrition delta) / 3. Most Area Three districts submitting plans followed the QIS format with monthly, quarterly, and annual awards for individual, team, and manager excellence. Bonus points were a feature in all districts. One district appears to reward only individual performance.

- Area Five, in the midwest, created an Area Incentive System (AIS) depending on an areawide formula for computing points and awarding bonus points. The plan targeted non-prior service, black upper mental group contracts, and new contract goal attained. Districts were encouraged to develop plans promoting high AIS scores.

- Area Eight created the Production Excellence Program (PEP), now called ACE, to uniformly and equitably evaluate and reward recruiting at all levels. It is the only authorized competition system in the area; however, noncompetitive local incentive programs continue. Production points are based on new contracts, emphasis points, bonus points, and workforce. The point calculations reward low attrition rates. Similar formulas with different definitions of variables apply for district, zone, and station competitions. The area also awards as many as 13 points to individual recruiters who write contracts at a specified level in the categories listed below:

New contract objective = 6 points

Workforce = 2 points

Upper mental group = 2 points

Black upper mental group = 1 point

Hispanic upper mental group = 1 point

Asian/Pacific Islander upper mental group = 1 point

Nuclear field = 1 point

These plans change as category emphasis and other recruiting factors change. The points help district commanders to track individual and district standings and are used to develop interdistrict competition strategies for the rewards such as the Admiral's Cup and other top recruiting awards. Many districts "game the system" by knowing the most valuable contracts and how goal emphasis may change during the year. For example, a district commander who can anticipate a change in category value can weight his district to be prepared and have a backlog of contracts in that category.[20]

THE FUTURE

A new national competition system is under development. Although area commanders are generally satisfied with creating and managing their own competitions, the national command wants more control over setting priorities. A national point system is also seen as more equitable for all recruiters. In a national system, rewards are thought to be more consistent with national priorities and the need to meet a goal. At the time of this writing, the new system was not sufficiently developed to include here.

---

[20]Based on various telephone conversations with Recruiting Command staff during 1995.

4. AIR FORCE

The Air Force has had two formal incentive systems since the early 1970s to encourage recruiters to meet and exceed annual recruiting goals. The Competition System was in effect through FY93 to stimulate groups and squadrons[1] to recruit in several enlistment categories, referred to as "programs." Programs in the Competition System include, for example, contracts written, accessions, enlistments into specific professions (e.g., physician or nurse), and Reserve Officer Training Corps (ROTC). Each program had its own point value for a contract written or an accession. That value was based on how difficult it was to enlist recruits, how important the category was to the performance of the Air Force mission, and how many contracts were required to maintain force size. The highest reward in this system was national recognition as annual Top Group and Top Squadron. The Annual Competition System was regulated by Headquarters, Air Force Recruiting Service (HQ/AFRS) until the start of FY94, when groups and their associated squadrons assumed responsibility for designing individualized competitions.

The second system, the Recruiting Service Incentive Awards Program, rewards the accomplishments of groups and squadrons participating in the Competition System, and it also provides awards to flights and individuals who are the best nationwide or who meet other specified criteria. These awards can be plaques, trophies, trips, watches, and other prizes. Examples of categories rewarded include Top Group, Top Squadron, Top Recruiter, Top Civilian, the Blue Suit Program, and other special bonus categories determined annually.

In addition to the annual competition and awards, different command levels use the two systems to create special short-term incentives as needed to meet short-term requirements such as seasonal shortfalls. For

---

[1]The reporting hierarchy of command moves from Headquarters Air Force Recruiting Service (HQ/AFRS) down to recruiting groups (of which there are four), to squadrons (28 as of January 1, 1996), and then to flights and recruiting stations (single- or multiple-person field offices for production recruiters and supervisors).

these short-term or bonus incentives, points or goal achievement may be used as the primary measure of success.

Both systems are responsive to the recruiting system structure. Individual recruiters can write or refer contracts in most programs, but they usually specialize in one type of recruit, such as non-prior service, officer training school, and health professions. Therefore, points are given and awards are presented both in the specialty categories and for combined overall performance.

This section is based on information available as of early FY96. That information covered the Competition System through FY93 (when it was suspended) and the Awards Program through FY94. Supplemental information for FY94 to FY96 is incorporated when possible.

GOALS

Air Force recruiting goals are determined as follows. First, Headquarters Air Force, with the assistance of the Surgeon General, the Office of Enlisted Programs, and other personnel program managers, determines annual force requirements in different categories such as health care, enlisted force, officer training programs, and others. Specific recruitment goals, that is, the number of recruits necessary to assure that the annual force size is maintained, are established to fill these requirements. The goals are then communicated to Recruiting Services Operations (RSO), which calculates appropriate allocations by group in each category, along with suggested squadron goals. Group goals are determined by statistical computations such as regression and weighted formulas.[2] RSO assigns allocations to groups, which in turn determine squadron goals. Squadrons assign monthly goals to flights, and goals for individuals are assigned at the squadron level by the squadron commander or program manager.

Each squadron is given a goal for writing contracts in a particular recruiting specialty (for example, physicians), as well as assigned

---

[2]Some factors that may be included in the calculations are available recruiting eligible population, mental test scores, vocational test scores, physical exam pass rates, state crime data, economic data by squadron, education levels, market characteristics, minority population characteristics, and prior recruiting performance.

goals in other categories (such as ROTC applications written, or referrals to other specialties).[3] Squadrons in the same group may have different assigned goals, depending on the group's overall goals. For example, a squadron located primarily in a large metropolitan area would probably have larger health professions and minority enlisted goals than a squadron located in a rural area.

COMPETITION SYSTEM

As discussed above, the national Competition System, in effect except for FY94, awards points as incentives to groups and squadrons for writing enlistment contracts or applications in specific program categories. The programs, and the categories included in each, are listed below.[4] The years that they were in use are shown in Appendix F (Table F.1).[5]

Enlisted programs

- Non-prior-service accessions
- Non-prior-service contracts
- Prior-service accessions
- Officer Training School (OTS) programs
- Black officer training school applications
- Minority officer training school applications
- Hispanic ROTC (FY95)
- Black ROTC
- ROTC scholarship applications
- Student vocational aptitude tests administered

---

[3]Assigned goals are all goals that must be met in addition to the specialty program. Another goal set, "non-assigned goals," includes some special minority categories and short-term incentive programs in which points are awarded or a reward is available if the goal is met. However, these non-assigned goals are not usually key performance measures.

[4]Officer programs are omitted. The categories, along with the criteria that must be met to win an award, will be described more fully in the Awards Program section.

[5]FY95 points are included for reference, although the competition system is not discussed.

- Nonscholarship referrals
- Eligible scholarship programs
- Combat controllers/parachute jumpers
- Basic military training attrition--male and female
- Ship day cancellations

Health professions

- Physicians
- Physician specialists
- Nurses
- Nurse specialists
- Allied health professions (AH)
- Dentists
- Medical service corps (Biomedical Sciences Corps--BSC)
- Health programs scholarship programs
- Physician assistant (PA) / physical therapist (PT)
- Biomedical sciences (BSC)

Commander emphasis

- Minority officer training accessions
- Physician assistant (PA) / physical therapist (PT)
- FY90 (February-September) mental category I accessions (high quality)
- Flight success
- Operation ASAP (Actively Seeking Another Provider)--FY92
- Activity Watch '92
- Mechanical Guaranteed Training Enlistment Program (GTEP) or mechanical aptitude index (AI)
- Black officer training school applications

Bonus points

- 100 percent in programs where 100 percent achievement is not the standard
- Physicians
- Nurse Specialists
- ROTC nurse scholarship applications

Assigning and Calculating Points

Each year, Recruiting Service Headquarters announced all the point values and the requirements for earning points. Headquarters was able to establish program priority by annually adjusting the point values. Each group and squadron was assigned a goal and received points for its recruiting efforts. Alone or in combination with other criteria, depending on the year, a group or squadron needed to have the highest point ranking or the highest program score to win. When more than one unit achieved the same point total, the winner was decided using a system of tie breakers that will be discussed below.

The point values assigned to categories each year reflected how well program and overall goals were met in the previous year, and how crucial each program was to filling vacancies and meeting goals in the current year. Appendix F shows points by program categories. Points were expressed in terms of weights multiplied by percentage achievement of category goals. The points in a category were awarded if the unit met an assigned goal or produced additional contracts beyond a program goal, i.e., overproduced. A total of 100 points were divided among the categories. To illustrate how points were calculated, consider a hypothetical enlisted program in which the goal is 20 enlistments with a point assignment of 16. Thirty enlistments are achieved, and therefore, 150 percent of goal. The 16 points are multiplied by 150 percent (1.5) for a total of 24.

For point assignment, each program category listed above was assigned a level of emphasis, in descending order: Across the Board (ATB), goaled, or no special emphasis.[6] Programs designated ATB were the highest in terms of points and included physician, nurse, BSC, and non-prior-service contracts. The points for these top categories ranged from 8 to 25, depending on the type of program (health, enlisted, etc:)

---

[6]For most of FY92, two emphasis levels were added. An emphasis level for physician and BSC enlistments was created, ranking above ATB; these categories were assigned 25 and 22 points, respectively. Also, only in FY92, there was a level for three target programs that were aimed at blacks and reserve officer training enlistments. These programs received one or two points. Other program points were adjusted to accommodate the new emphasis levels.

and year. Achieving all ATB program goals was required for competition in the next level, goaled programs.

Goaled programs included all ATB categories (and counted those where points were achieved), all health professions, and most enlisted programs (such as contracts written, accessions, students tested, ROTC applications and OTS applications). Goaled programs changed slightly each year, but usually included eleven or twelve program categories. Points for the non-ATB programs ranged from 2 to 7.

Each year, the Recruiting Service Commander reserved four or five of the 100 points to use as special bonus incentives for hard-to-fill or special-need categories. For instance, in FY92, the Commander added a PA/PT category to the ATB program and awarded his five points to the new category. There were small yearly variations, but by and large, enlistment categories selected remained stable.

Points were determined cumulatively as contracts were written.[7] Flights applied the point values, tallied them, and then reported them to squadrons, which reported them to groups for final calculations before submission to headquarters for final ranking. Points were reported to squadrons and groups in varying time frames (by the month, quarterly, semiannually, or yearly, depending on the Commander), but HQ/AFRS automatically translated report categories into cumulative averages for the year.

Breaking Ties and Determining Award Winners

When more than one unit achieved the same Competition System point total in any program or category and no clear winner emerged, final standings were determined using a set of criteria called determinants (or "tiebreakers"). The criteria were applied successively until final standings were resolved. Although the determinants were altered through

---

[7]In FY93, for only that year, point matrices based on an exponential "S" curve were developed for calculating point awards. This means that the number of points for each additional contract increased slower than they would have with a linear increase. Using this method, points were capped at a certain level (usually between 130 percent and 200 percent) to promote recruiting activity in all programs.

the years, they generally included four criteria that were calculated in order as follows:

1. Number of ATB programs where 100 percent or more of goal was achieved,
2. Number of goaled programs where 100 percent or more of goal was achieved,
3. Total points for all programs, and
4. Percentage of goal accomplished in the highest-point program.

At the final step to break ties, the percentage accomplished in the two highest-point programs was calculated, and if the tie remained, this process would continue adding successively lower-point programs until the tie was broken. Determinants were applied as tiebreakers whenever a tie occurred in any program or category. It is notable that points, as a tiebreaker for ranking, were considered third after the highest-value contract programs, i.e., ATB and goaled programs. Determinants were eliminated at the national level beginning in FY93, though some recruiting groups subsequently reinstated them in their own plans.

To receive awards, winners first had to meet required criteria in Awards Program categories, and then be designated by Recruiting Service Headquarters as the best or "top" in that category. For example, the winning Top Enlisted Group between March 1992 and the beginning of FY94 was required to meet the following criteria:

1. Achieve overall goal for all components of the enlisted program.
2. Achieve the highest Competition System score for the enlisted program, and
3. Achieve enlistment goal in the following specific enlisted program components: contracts, accessions, students tested, ROTC, ROTC black, OTS, and OTS minority applications.

Competition in FY94

As of the end of FY93, the Air Force terminated the national-level competition system, hoping to give field commanders the autonomy to determine recruiting priorities and emphasize or promote undersubscribed categories. The new system also provided group and lower-level commanders the opportunity to reward individuals and offices for their response to incentives.

Each group was free to use whatever system or set of requirements it felt would provide the proper incentives to achieve or exceed goal allocations. Each group developed its own set of points that reflected goals, markets, and recruiter knowledge and abilities. However, most groups chose to award points within a structure similar to the earlier national Competition System, rather than to develop new systems. The group system designs ranged from a simple Group Commander regulation to individual squadron plans with their own point systems and complete guidelines. For example, one squadron required flight-level plans for points and rewards. Some groups created semiannual, quarterly, and monthly programs as well as adding targeted flight programs. One recruiting group assigned points to eleven categories such as physician, nurse, and net reservations (contracts), and it required that at least 100 percent of the goal be attained before any points were awarded. Seven other categories, such as minority ROTC, nurse specialist, and medical service corps, were rewarded for a portion of goal. In the OTS program, subgoals with point awards for overproduction were designated in the minority black and minority Hispanic programs. Another group chose to subtract points for not meeting specified program criteria.

As in previous years, achievement was rewarded by way of the Awards Program as well as in smaller local competitions. A squadron from each group was nominated for top ranking at the end of each year. The Top Group award category was eliminated, but groups still received awards for specific enlistment categories such as Top Enlisted Program, Top Health Professions Team, and Group Mission Accomplishment. These awards were presented through the Awards Program by all command levels, including headquarters, groups, squadrons, and flights.

The less centralized recruiter incentive systems in effect for FY94 were reevaluated. The Air Force decided to reinstate a national Competition System beginning in FY95 and published revised instructions.

AWARDS PROGRAM

The Recruiting Service Incentive Awards Program establishes criteria and awards to motivate recruiters, enhance morale, and promote successful recruiting.[8] All groups, squadrons, flights, Military Entrance Processing Stations (MEPS) personnel, individual recruiters, supervisory personnel, civilian personnel, and spouses may compete where appropriate. Awards are presented for group, squadron, and individual performance in numerous categories, as shown in Appendix G.[9] The criteria for winning awards are diverse and can also be reviewed in those tables. Many group and squadron awards are based on Competition System points and other criteria; for others, goal achievement, or some other subjective criteria, such as recruiter ability or recruiting markets, are the primary achievement indicators.

Incorporated in the program are awards for Competition System group and squadron winners. Also incorporated are Air Force Recruiting Command Incentive Sub-Programs (described below), such as Operation Blue Suit, Master and Senior Recruiter Badge, and Recruiting Service Olympiad. Additionally, the Commander may offer one-time awards programs that have definite beginning and end dates during the year as special needs arise. Examples of these one-time Commander incentives (presented in Appendix H) are the Operation ASAP, Activity Watch '92, and Mechanical GTEP (training program for jet engine methanics) or AI programs.

Many awards are presented to individual recruiters for their accomplishments. These recruiters track their progress and compete for rewards in a variety of programs implemented at the squadron or flight level. Usually, recruiters are assigned goals by their squadron or flight supervisor. The standard is 2 or 3 new recruits per month per recruiter, plus any special-need requirements such as mobilizations or specialty program shortages. When selecting recruiters for awards, most

---

[8]This program, adjusted annually, has existed throughout the time period covered here.

[9]As shown in Table G.3, Awards Programs measure annual FY performance, but new regulations are issued only periodically when revisions are implemented. Therefore, Tables G.1, G.2, and G.3 display information conforming to the dates on regulations rather than by FY.

squadrons or flights consider either percentage of goal achieved or
status in a squadron or flight point system. The point systems are
unique to each unit, unlike the national competition system, and are
used by the unit for competition, record keeping, and local awards. To
receive an award in the Awards Program, a recruiter is selected by the
squadron commander, after which a nomination, including required
documentation of accomplishment, is submitted to headquarters.
Individual recruiters also compete in local flight or station incentive
activities that are not the subject of this report.

Categories, Criteria, and Awards

Each awards category has specified requirements the winner must
satisfy. The more than thirty awards are diverse and encompass numerous
recruiting activities, such as Squadron Mission Accomplishment, Top
Safety Program, Top Rookie, Top Supervisor, and Top Civilian of the
Year. To receive an award, the groups and squadrons usually need to
have the highest Competition System score overall or in a program
category. Often they also must have 100 percent goal attainment in all
other assigned goals. This creates an incentive for fulfilling overall
contract goal requirements. Some programs have their own unique
criteria as well, which must also be met if an award is to be presented.

Over the years, awards categories and criteria have changed in
response to changing conditions. For example, in the group awards, when
the Medical Service Corps program was all but eliminated in FY93, the
physician category was incorporated into the Top Medical category. In
FY94, when groups assumed responsibility for setting incentive targets,
point requirements were changed to other criteria, e.g., production,
special emphasis, and discretionary ways to look at quality.

One set of awards, given in the Annual Standard of Excellence
Program, is designed to encourage overproduction in the Competition
System by groups and squadrons. To win one of these awards, goal and
over-goal achievement (rather than points) are required, as shown in
Appendix G. All groups and squadrons achieving the criteria are given
awards. In some programs, particularly in health-related categories,

recruiters compete either in the individual categories or as squadron teams. When team awards are presented, each member receives an award.

Several types of awards are presented to the winners. Most recruiting achievement in the Awards Program is rewarded officially with plaques and trophies that may be presented individually or at awards ceremonies. Awards based on the Competition System, for example, are typically plaques.[10] Often, additional recruiting service gifts such as watches, briefcases, clocks, or business card cases are presented to individuals (at the discretion of the unit commander) for their achievement. Trips to Recruiting Service Command presentation ceremonies or planned vacation leaves reward particularly high performance from units or individuals.

Special Incentive Programs

The Blue Suit, Senior and Master Recruiting Badge programs, and the Recruiting Service Olympiad are four annual Awards Program incentive programs sponsored by the Recruiting Service. They are promoted in recruiting units because they seek to stimulate overproduction with prestigious awards.

- **Operation Blue Suit** is the Recruiting Commander's special incentive program. The program was initiated in 1979 to reward the annual Top Flight recruiters and supervisors. In 1988, after flights from the same highly productive market area dominated the award, the program was changed to honor at least two recruiters in each group. The group commander selects one awardee and submits two additional nominations to the Commander's selection board (1 Colonel and 2 senior noncommissioned officers). The winners and their spouses are invited to Headquarters in San Antonio for a week of entertainment.

- **Senior and Master Recruiting Badges** (or Silver and Gold Badges, respectively) are overproduction awards presented to enlisted

---

[10]When Top Group was still a category before FY94, a rotating engraved bowl was presented in addition to a permanent plaque.

recruiters and their supervisors. Generally for both badges, recruiters and supervisors in all specialty categories except physician recruiter must be assigned a non-prior-service new contract individual goal by their squadron commander, and then must:

- achieve 100 percent of all assigned goals and 115 percent in contracts written,
- achieve a dropout rate of less than 15 percent by the time of accession to basic military training,
- produce at least 50 percent of accessions in AFQT mental categories I and II (added in FY95),
- be a production recruiter or supervisor for 12 full months in the competition year, and
- meet certain goal assignment criteria.

Physician recruiters qualify when 100 percent of the accession goal is achieved.[11] Supervisor badge criteria are similar to enlisted recruiters but are applied to the entire unit (e.g., flight achieves 100 percent of all assigned goals and 115 percent of non-prior-service enlisted new contracts).

Non-prior-service (NPS) flight supervisors are the only award recipients who must meet a recruit quality component.[12] To

_____

[11]When recruiters began working in teams to recruit in the medical and nurse categories, team overproduction criteria were established for each category. All members of winning teams receive a Senior Recruiting Badge and are eligible for a Masters Badge.

[12]Generally there were few recruit quality indicators in the Recruiting Service incentive programs, because Air Force recruits are required to place very high on the AFQT. Scores are targeted in AFQT category I and II (around 65 or greater). New recruits must at the least be high school graduates.

In FY90, a non-goaled Non-Prior-Service Accessions category was added to the Competition System. This category awarded 3 points for a recruit entering active duty and scoring in AFQT category I (top 7 percent). The Commander also added a bonus of 2 points for category I accessions between February and September 1990.

In response to current changes in required applicant AFQT scores, one group developed a six-month program to increase category I and II applications by rewarding the squadron with the greatest percentage of increase.

achieve this award, the supervisor must preside over a flight that enlists 50 percent or better in AFQT mental categories I and II. All badge-eligible recruiters in the flight must also achieve 100 percent of goal and record less than a 15 percent Basic Military Training (BMT) attrition rate.

The Master Recruiter Badge may be awarded annually, at the discretion of the squadron commander, to one individual in each squadron who previously received a Senior Badge and meets all those criteria as described above and all criteria established by the squadron in its individual awards directives.

- The **Recruiting Service Olympiad** is a program to reward high-volume recruiters for making non-prior-service active duty enlistments each fiscal year. Bronze, silver, and gold medals are awarded within guidelines established annually. Until 1992, gold medal winners were required to enlist at least 100 new recruits. Upon discovering inequalities between force reduction goals and the Olympiad requirements, HQ/AFRS reduced the gold medal target to 80 or more recruits and also revised the other medal categories accordingly. The names of individuals producing 100 or more active duty enlistments are permanently engraved on the "Century Club" plaque. Exact targets for all categories and years can be found in Appendix G.

Recruiting Service and Group Commander Emphasis and Bonus Programs

Each fiscal year, Recruiting Service and recruiting group commanders are free to add emphasis or bonus programs as needed. These are listed in Table 4.1 (see also Appendix F). The recruiting group programs were announced in periodic bulletins and awards were presented in the groups.

Table 4.1

Recruiting Service and Group Commander Emphasis and Bonus Programs

Fiscal Year	Command[a]	Program	Award
FY88	RS	Minority officer training school	Double points
FY89	RS	Black officer training enlistments	Double points
FY90	RS	None cited	None cited
FY91	RS	Upper mental group category I	2 points
FY91	RS	Nurse Specialist	Double points
FY92	RS	PA/PT added to goaled program.	5 CO emphasis points
	RG	Magnificent 7, quarterly Top Enlisted	No data
FY93	RS	"Flight Success" bonus contracts (points could be subtracted if certain low point categories were not achieved)	5 points/mo/yr 13 opportunities
FY 94	RG	Spur net contracts = highest percentage over goal	Gifts and medals to 1 flight, flight members and flight supervisor
	RG	Bonus-recruiting physicians Galore in '94 5 top recruiters	5-10 points trip and gift
	RG	Flight non-prior-service applications for mental test category ≥ 90 or college graduate ≥ 65	Monthly plaque to flight, flight supervisor, and member top squadron
	RG	Reduce errors at military processing stations. Begin with 100 points and subtract errors. Highest score wins	Luxury trip to HQ
FY95	RS	Mechanical GTEP - AI (see Appendix H)	
	RG	Top net contracts - highest percentage over goal	Put in AFCM, trip

[a]RS = Recruiting Service; RG = recruiting group; CO = commander, AFCM = Air Force Commendation Medal.

5. MARINE CORPS

The Marine Corps Recruiting Service operates under a national incentive plan established in the late 1970s and early 1980s and a number of separate programs at regional and lower levels. The national plan has remained in effect, essentially unchanged, until the present time and is described in a draft five-volume set of guidebooks for recruiters, recruiting stations, and recruiting districts. The plan contains three national recruiter incentive programs--the Commandant's Enlisted Superior Achiever Awards for recruiting stations, and the Recruiter and Non-commissioned Officer of the Year Programs for one individual in each category. Some commandants have also initiated temporary programs to create incentives and reward recruiters. However, most recruiter incentive programs in the Marine Corps are created, managed, and rewarded at lower command levels.

This chapter describes national and regional programs and rewards for recruiters and recruiting units responsible for enlisted recruits. Reserve and officer programs are not included. Enlisted programs below the regional level are described in Appendix I. We begin with an outline of how the recruiting effort is organized, followed by a discussion of the recruiting goals that set the standards for recruiter production.

STAFF, COMMAND, AND ORGANIZATION

Unlike recruiters in the other military services, those in the Marine Corps are also responsible for selecting and selling enlistment contracts in specific job occupational fields.[1] This additional responsibility requires active recruiter participation with recruit applicants throughout the entire enlistment process, i.e., signing a contract, reporting to duty, and graduating from recruit training. Follow-through is emphasized and rewarded.

---

[1]In the Army, Air Force, and Navy, job counselors or MEPS liaisons are responsible for job or enlistment field selections.

The Commandant of the Marine Corps (CMC) is the overall authority for Marine Corps recruiting activities. The Marine Corps Recruiting Command is responsible for informing the CMC and drafting policy. Recruiting policy and goals are set, transmitted, and managed through the following hierarchy.

- Marine Corps Recruiting Command (MCRC) - A major general, known as the Commanding General MCRC, leads the Command, sets policies, and allocates missions (goals) to regions with recommendations for district allocations and performance standards.

- Recruiting Regions (RRs) - An East and West Region are each commanded by a brigadier general, who is responsible for recruiting in their respective region.

- Marine Corps Districts (MCDs) - Six districts are each commanded by a colonel who assigns missions and allocates personnel (structure) to the recruiting stations. The district commanding officer is assisted by an executive officer and an operations officer who both are usually lieutenant colonels.

- Recruiting Stations (RSs) - Currently there are 49 recruiting stations each commanded by a major who is responsible for achieving its assigned mission. These stations manage all aspects of the recruiting process.

- Recruiting Sub Stations (RSSs) - These are recruiting offices led by non-commissioned officers in charge (NCOIC). Currently there are 554 sub stations. They are the most numerous units, and fluctuate with recruiting requirements.

- Permanent Contact Stations (PCSs) - These offices are established in areas where there is heavy traffic such as shopping malls. PCSs may be collocated with other service offices and are manned full-time under the control of an NCOIC of a RSS.

- Transient Recruiting Facilities (TRFs) - To periodically work in outlying regions of an RSS's area of responsibility, a recruiting facility, manned on less than a full-time basis, is used by individual recruiters.

GOALS

Each fiscal year, a national Personnel Procurement Operation Plan (OPLAN) is prepared containing the annual and monthly contracts written and total force enlisted shipping requirements (i.e., required numbers reporting to recruit training) with shares allocated by region and suggestions for allocation by district.[2] Since recruits do not necessarily ship in the month they sign a contract, region commanders determine the number of new contracts required to assure that monthly shipping goals are satisfied. Commanders must also meet a national mandate that at least 55 percent of the year's shipping requirements be in the DEP at the beginning of each fiscal year.

The region apportions new contract goals to recruiting districts. Within these shipping and new contract goals, other goals for applicant education, quality, and racial and ethnic mix are established. Additionally, quotas and criteria are included for other goals (e.g., musicians), terms of enlistment, and over- and undershipment. Thus, the Marine plans emphasize the full recruiting process.

Individual recruiter goals are determined at each recruiting unit level to conform with the unit's assigned mission. Each recruiting sub-station non-commissioned officer in charge establishes daily work requirements to ensure that recruiters satisfy individually assigned missions.

AWARDS

A variety of awards may be earned through the incentive plans discussed in detail below. Some awards are promulgated by the Office of the CMC and are not specific to recruiting. These awards are shown in Table 5.1 in hierarchical order, with the highest status first. Usually, the first three awards go to higher-ranking Marines.

---

[2]Until FY94, the OPLAN was issued by the Commandant of the Marine Corps. Since FY94, the plan comes from Headquarters, Marine Corps Recruiting Command.

Table 5.1

**Marine Corps Awards and Recognition
in Hierarchical Order**

Award/ Recognition	Criteria	Command Level Presenting	Comments
Legion of Merit	Exceptionally meritorious conduct in performing outstanding service	Secretary of the Navy	
Meritorious Service Medal	Distinguished outstanding meritorious service or accomplishment	Commandant of the Marine Corps or authorized commander	
Navy Commendation Medal	Distinguished heroic or meritorious achievement	Authorized commander	Commandant issues certificate and commander awards it to the recruiter
Navy/Marine Corps Achievement Medal	Sustained performance or specific achievement of a superlative nature as an individual or leader	Commanders authorized to convene special courts martial	These may be district level or higher; awarded to major or lower rank
Certificate of Commendation	Exceptional performance beyond normal expectations	Commandant of the Marine Corps	
Certificate of Commendation		Battalion commander or equivalent	
Meritorious Mast	Noteworthy, commendable, or innovative service beyond normal expectations	Same as Achievement Medal (or commanding general)	Usually presented to sergeants or below
Letter of Appreciation	Noteworthy or commendable performance	Any officer senior to recipient	Not put into personnel file

SOURCES: Navy and Marine Corps Awards Manual, SECNAVINST 1650.1F, August 8, 1991, and various district awards and recognition instructions.

The awards shown in Table 5.1 are based on the general criteria given, which can be adapted to different commands such as the Marine Corps Recruiting Command. Awards are presented based on either a specific act or achievement or sustained superior performance. Superior

performance awards usually are issued at the end of each FY. In the
MCRC, these awards can be presented at the discretion of either the
commanding general or local commander for performance in special
recruiting campaigns or for overall success. Different recruiting
levels are authorized to present each of the awards shown in Table 5.1.

Other forms of recruiting force recognition, including material
awards, may be earned through the MCRC incentive plans. Promotion
incentives, for example, may be included in the plans, but they are
emphasized to a lesser extent than in the other services. The awards
are described in the context of each plan.

RECRUITING INCENTIVE PLANS

National Plan

For many years, Headquarters, Marine Corps Recruiting Command,
administered only the Commandant's Superior Achiever Award for top
recruiting stations and periodic short-term campaigns to reward
recruiting units and individuals. Awards were added in FY95 for the top
national recruiter as Recruiter of the Year, and in FY96 for Non-
commissioned Officer of the Year.

The Commandant's Superior Achiever Awards are presented to
recruiting stations for meeting and exceeding annual quantity and
quality goals in a "superlative" manner. Recruiting stations are
recommended by district commanders to their region command. The
regional commander reviews these recommendations and then nominates
deserving stations to the Commandant. The number of stations receiving
the Superior Achiever Award is not limited. Selected recruiting
stations receive their awards at the annual Recruiting Operations and
Training Conference. In addition to this public recognition, the
winning stations each receive a letter from the Commandant and a large
plaque portraying a brass etched copy of the letter. These plaques are
displayed at the recruiting station.

Over the years the criteria have changed slightly, but the FY95
plan is representative of the overall requirements necessary to qualify

for the award.[3]   (Table 5.2 illustrates ways the plan has changed since 1987.)   The criteria for the FY95 plan include:

1. OPLAN requirements must be met or exceeded,

2. Standards and criteria must be satisfied as objectively as possible,

3. Automated Recruiting Management System (ARMS) data must be used to complete the nomination worksheet,[4]

4. At least 100 percent of recruiting station goals must be met,

5. At least 90 percent of non-prior-service enlistments must be 4-, 5-, and 6-year terms,

6. Shipped persons must be at least 95 percent high school graduates and 63 percent in mental categories I-IIIA,

7. The musician goal must be achieved, and

8. The next-year DEP must be at least 55 percent filled. At least 95 percent of those in the pool must be high school graduates, and 63 percent must be in mental categories I-IIIA.

Recruiter and NCOIC of the Year. Created in FY95, this award honors one recruiter each year who is chosen from among six nominated (one from each district). All active duty or extended reserve recruiters who write contracts during the full FY are eligible for nomination.

The nominated recruiters are required to:

- meet height, weight and physical fitness standards,
- complete education requirements for promotion,
- perform with direct effect on mission success, and
- get 63% of their contracts in mental category I-IIIA, 95 percent from high school graduates, with no more than 20 percent shipping pool attrition and 13 percent region depot attrition.

---

[3]Source: *Personnel Procurement OPLAN, FY95*, Commanding General, Marine Corps Recruiting and Recruit Training Command, September 23, 1994.

[4]ARMS is a Marine Corps recruiting data collection system.

Table 5.2

Commandant's Superior Achiever Award Criteria, FY 87 to FY 95:
Percent Enlisted Recruits Required

Award Criteria	Fiscal Year								
	87	88	89	90	91	92	93	94	95
Shipping goal[a]									
Male mission	100	100	100	100	100	100	100	100	100
Female mission	100	100	100	100	100	100	100	100	100
Total force	100	100	100	100	100	100	100	100	100
Shipping quality[a, b]									
Male non-prior-service high school graduate[c]	95	90	90	90	95	95	95	95	95
Male non-prior-service mental category I-IIIA	63	63							
Male and female non-prior-service mental category I-IIIA			63	63	64	64	63	63	63
Shipping criteria									
Term of enlistment 4, 5, or 6 years[b]	90	90	90	90	90	90	90	90	90
College Enlistment Program & Quality Enlistment Program combined[a]	100								
Quota serial number filled[a]						100	100	100	100
Shipping pool[a]									
Total force starting pool	50	50	50	55	60	65	55	55	55
Reserve Officer Training Scholarships[a]	100	100	100	100	100	100	100	100	100
Musician Enlistment Option Program[a]					100	100	100	100	100

NOTE: Winners must also satisfy reserve criteria and quotas. Quotas are the goals assigned to recruiting stations by the recruiting district.

[a]Percentage of goal that must be achieved.

[b]Percentage of contracts or recruits shipped that must meet the characteristics stated.

[c]From 1988 on must be high school graduates in the highest qualification test level (Tier I).

The winner is recognized for exceptional leadership, management, organization ability, innovation, and initiative in accomplishing the mission. In addition to recognition, the top recruiter receives a Navy

Commendation Medal from the Commandant and a promotion to the next-higher rank. The five nominees not selected receive the same medal from the Commanding General of the Marine Corps Recruiting Command.

Non-commissioned Officer in Charge of the Year. Recently created, this new program recognizes NCOICs in addition to recruiters. The nominated NCOIC must satisfy all the recruiter requirements and must:

- lead the RSS to achieve 100 percent of the assigned contract and shipping mission, and
- not have been previously selected as Marine Corps Recruiting Command or Marine Corps District NCOIC of the Year.

Each nominee receives a Navy and Marine Corps Commendation Medal from the Commanding General and a professional library. The nominee selected as NCOIC of the year also receives an award from the Marine Corps Association.

The Summer Recruiting Offensive of 1989: A Commandant's Campaign

Periodically, a Commandant designs and initiates incentive programs with awards bestowed at the national or local level. These programs usually have a specified term and focus that encourages efforts for a special need or in a category requiring an extra push. One example is the Summer Recruiting Offensive conducted in 1989.

In June of that year, the Commandant circulated an instruction for a campaign to reward individual recruiters and units. This program lasted for two months, from July 1 to August 31, and focused on placing high-quality recruits in the October-to-May DEP.[5] The expected result was to increase high-quality contracts and to prepare the DEP for a transition to a monthly 10 percent level load shipping pattern.[6] Participants in the offensive included recruiters, non-commissioned

---

[5]Instruction # 1500 MRT, 15 June 1989.

[6]Level load shipping was originally designed to ship the same number of recruits each month. This plan did not fit into the recruiting cycle (it did not allow for seasonal and other differences) and was revised to increase the variance allowed around 10 percent. Currently, a FY trimester shipping goal is in effect, so 32 percent ship the first trimester, 22 percent ship the second trimester, and 46 percent ship in the last trimester of the FY.

officers, recruiting station commanders, district directors, and recruiting units.

Requirements. Individuals and recruiting units were measured by the gross number of high-quality contracts written that met occupational fields assigned in the mission. Recruiters were handicapped based on their previous production levels by creating high and low performance groups.[7] In addition, recruiting sub-stations were handicapped as large and small.[8] The handicaps were designed to create an incentive for all recruiters to compete.

Awards. Awards were presented at the national, district, and recruiting station level. Each level incorporated 1st, 2nd, and 3rd place winners resulting in over 40 awards. The prizes included framed, autographed posters of the Commandant, Certificates of Commendation, leather flight jackets, swords, and autographed baseball bats.

In addition to the awards just described, the Commandant presented special awards to top producers during the campaign period. The recruiter in each district who wrote the most gross contracts received a Navy Achievement Medal. The non-commissioned recruiting sub-station officer in charge of the sub-station with the most gross contracts in each district was awarded a Navy Achievement Medal, and the NCOIC with the most gross contracts in the region was nominated for meritorious promotion. Another special award went to poolees (people who sign contracts and are awaiting shipment) who refer potential recruits to recruiters. They received a Commandant's poster for two referrals or a Marine Corps buckle for three referrals.

Western Recruiting Region Plan

The Western Region Decoration and Awards Program currently in effect is designed to reward "meritorious performance, outstanding acts of heroism, achievement, and sustained superior performance" by

---

[7]Recruiters averaging two or more contracts per month before the campaign competed against each other and recruiters with less than two contracts competed against each other.

[8]Large recruiting sub-stations had four or more recruiters and small ones had less than four.

recruiting units and individuals.[9] This plan provides for awards
bestowed by the region and awards that districts may use for their
incentive programs.

Requirements and Awards. There are four specific western region
incentive awards programs for sustained performance with superior
results:

1. Top recruiting station,
2. Most improved recruiting station,
3. NCOIC and recruiter of the year, and
4. Quality award.

The top recruiting station of the year must ship 100 percent of its
mission in each category (males, females, ROTC scholarships, etc.),
produce 100 percent of the CMC's new contract goals, and not exceed a
set attrition level. Stations are ranked by average quantity and
quality of the recruits contracted and shipped, per recruiter. A bronze
statue of an eagle is awarded to the winning recruiting station.

The most improved recruiting station is judged by improvement in
quality and quantity attainment. Districts each nominate one station to
the region commander, who makes the final selection and awards a plaque.

Districts also nominate non-commissioned officers-in-charge and
recruiters for one annual award each—a plaque. The top NCOIC from the
entire western recruiting region receives an NCO sword.

There is also a quality award given to one recruiting station.
Station quality rankings are based on how well recruits are screened
before they are shipped and include percentage of recruits who report
for duty, who are high school graduates or in mental group categories
I-IIIA, who pass an initial physical-strength test, who pass urinalysis,
and who make no post-enlistment disclosures of certain kinds (drugs,
arrests, etc.). The achievement of each station in each category is
compiled in an automated system and ranked relative to all stations in
the district. Using these rankings, an awards board makes the final
selection and uses its discretion in the event of a tie. Usually the

---

[9]Depot Order 1650.7M, *Depot Decorations and Awards Program*, Western
Recruiting Region, 1992.

station with the lowest attrition percentage and best category I-IIIA percentage is selected.

Eastern Recruiting Region Plan

The Eastern Recruiting Region provides guidance, sets standards, and supports district and station recruiting and recruiter activities. To provide recruiter incentives, it administers the Commandant's Superior Achiever Award and periodically conducts regionwide award programs. Two examples of Eastern Recruiting Region recruiter incentive awards programs are the Superior Performance Award in 1995 and the Triple Crown War Club Award in 1996. For 1996, an overall recruiter incentive plan was also in force.

FY95. All recruiting stations meeting Eastern Recruiting Region recruit quality and quantity goals during FY95 were recognized and awarded the Superior Performance Award. Those stations also qualified for Eastern Recruiting Region Station of the Year. Stations must achieve the following five awards criteria:

1. FY shipping mission,
2. FY contracting goal,
3. Prescribed start pool,
4. Prescribed I-IIIA shipping and contracting percentages, and
5. Prescribed Tier I shipping and contracting percentages.

Each eligible recruiting station that met all standards for all five criteria listed above received a Commanding General's Certificate of Commendation as the Superior Performance Award. The recruiting station with the best attrition percentage for the FY was awarded a trophy as Eastern Recruiting Region Station of the Year. Attrition percentage represents overall contracting quality and training preparation factors.

FY96. The Eastern Recruiting Region FY96 award and recognition plan includes an overall plan and a Triple Crown War Club Award plan. The overall commanding general's plan contains four initiatives to reward district and recruiting station commanders, and recruiters. The

Triple Crown War Club Award emphasizes recruiting station shipping, contracting, and quality attainment.

Overall plan criteria and awards are as follows:

1. All district and recruiting station commanders achieving monthly contract goals receive a congratulatory call from the commanding general.

2. Each month, the recruiting station commander with the highest region contract attainment receives a letter of congratulation from the commanding general.

3. Each month, the recruiting station commander with the highest district contract attainment receives a letter of congratulations from the commanding general.

4. Recruiters of the top male and female recruit graduating from training attend graduation as the commanding general's guest. Graduations are weekly events.

The Triple Crown War Club Awards go each month to the top recruiting station that achieves all of the following:

1. Lowest region attrition overall (the award is not given if the station exceeds the region's fiscal year-to-date attrition),
2. Overall shipping mission, and
3. Net new contract mission.

The award for this plan is an engraved Louisville Slugger baseball bat.

District and Station Plans

Each district devises an overall plan offering incentives and awards to recruiters and recruiting units for meeting or surpassing . goals and performance standards. These plans usually are based on point schemes that emphasize recruiting priorities. Priorities differ somewhat among districts, depending on their assigned goals. Often, short-term campaigns are devised to provide additional incentives during specific seasons or to meet key goals. Generally, these campaigns have a theme that generates enthusiasm and focuses recruiter attention.

Depending on the scope of the plan and the expected outcome, success could be measured by overall or specific category point achievement, goal achievement, quality achievement, and/or contract quantity achievement. The awards have varied in number; usually, there have been awards for units (by size) and individuals. Depending on the rigor of the competition, awards could include medals, certificates, plaques, swords, trophies, letters, and gift items.[10] Some short-term incentive plans that focused primarily on the number of contracts written used symbols from sports, the wild west and cowboys, or the Marine Corps as themes. They used titles such as Superbowl 96, Ghost Rider 95, and Operation Southern Storm. Other campaigns with titles such as Grizzly Award, Operation Balanced Excellence, and Buffalo Hunt focused on at least two of the following: contracts written, high school graduates, mental quality, shipping and shipping pools, or recruiting unit quality. Two examples of district plans during the 1990s appear in Appendix I.

Stations developed plans that rewarded recruiters and NCOICs for achievement in categories similar to those in the district plans. Awards in these plans were usually trophies, plaques, certificates, medals, and gift items such as mugs or t-shirts.

---

[10]The western region allocates 130 Navy Achievement Medals to its three districts to use for their incentive programs.

6. CONCLUSION

We have described the incentive plans and goaling methods used by the services over the past 15 years or so to manage their recruiting personnel. We have shown that different services have taken different approaches and, even within a service, the approach has varied over time. The plans have varied in terms of their emphasis on units or individual behavior, the method used to measure performance, whether absolute or relative performance is used as a basis for rewards, and whether the incentive systems are run at the national or more local levels. The frequency of changes suggests that the services themselves are unclear as to what incentive plan best fits their needs in any given set of circumstances. Although some past research has examined how goals and some specific incentive plan features have affected recruiter behavior, relatively little is still known about the answers to such questions as:

1. Has productivity been increased because of changes in service incentive plans?
2. Is one plan better than another?
3. What features should the ideal plan have?
4. If one plan is clearly more effective, should OSD direct a standardized incentive plan?
5. Are monetary incentives feasible?

Answering these questions requires several inputs. First, one needs a model of recruiter behavior and how it responds to various factors, including incentives. Second, one needs empirical estimates based on this model that will indicate how recruiter behavior and therefore recruiting outcomes respond to alternative incentive plan features. Although past research has provided some insights into how recruiter behavior responds to incentive systems, that earlier work did not take a broad approach. It did not address such issues as whether competitive or relative performance standards are better than criterion-based or absolute performance standards, whether plans based on unit performance are better than ones based on individual performance, and so forth. Future research should provide these inputs. In doing so, it will also provide insight into how incentive systems affect recruiting outcomes, and whether changes in these systems can account in an important way for problems that arise in meeting accession targets.

Appendix A

ARMY INCENTIVE AWARD POINTS

Table A.1

Regular Army Incentive Award Points[1]

FY YR	FY QTR	MO	GSA, CA, PPV	GSA, CA, OPV	GSB, CB, PPV	GSB, CB, OPV	PSA PPV	PSA OPV	PSB PPV	PSB OPV	HA PPV	HA OPV	G4 PPV	G4 OPV	NA PPV	NA OPV	HB PPV	HB OPV	S4 PPV	S4 OPV	N4&H4 PPV	N4&H4 OPV	NB PPV	NB OPV	PA PPV	PA OPV	PB PPV	PB OPV	Other
95	1		30/20²																										
94³	4		40	70	20	30	30	50			5	5	5	5	5	5			10	10			5	5			10	20	10
94	3		20	60	10	30	10	20	10	20	5	10	5	5	5	5	5	5									10	20	
94	2		20	60	10	30	10	20	10	20	5	10	5	5	5	5	5	5											
94	1		20	60	10	30					5	15	5	10	5	5	5	5											
93	3 & 4		20	60	10	30					5	15	5	10	5	5	5	5							10	20	10	20	
93	2		20	60	10	30					5	15	5	10	5	5	5	5							10	20	10	20	
93	1		20	60	10	30					5	15	5	10	5	5	5	5							10	20	10	20	
92	4		20	50	10	20					5	10			5	10									5	10	5	10	
92	3		20	50	10	20					5	10			5	10									5	10	5	10	
92	2		20	50	10	20					5	10			5	10									5	10	5	10	
92	1		20	50	10	20					5	10			5	10									5	10	5	10	
91	4	Sep	20	40 60	10	20					5	10			5	10									5	10	5	10	
91	4	Aug	20	40 60	10	20					5	10			5	10									5	10	5	10	
91	4	Jul	20	40 60	10	20					5	10			5	10									5	10	5	10	
91	3	Jun	20	40 60	10	20					5	10			5	10									5	10	5	10	
91	3	May	20	40 60	10	20					5	10			5	10									5	10	5	10	
91	2	Mar	20	40 60	5	10					5	10			5	10									5	10	5	10	
91	2	Feb	20	40 60	5	10					5	10			5	10									5	10	5	10	
91	2	Jan	20	40 60	5	10					5	10			5	10									5	10	5	10	
91	1	Dec	20	40 60	5	10					5	10			5	10									5	10	5	10	
91	1	Nov	20	40 60	5	10					5	10			5	10									5	10	5	10	
91	1	Oct	20	40 60	5	10					5	10			5	10									5	10	5	10	
90	4	Sep	20	40 60	5	10					5	10			5	10									5	10	5	10	
90	4	Aug	20	40 60	5	10					5	10			5	10									5	10	5	10	
90	4	Jul	20	40 60	5	10					5	10			5	10									5	10	5	10	
90	3	Jun	20	40 60	5	10					5	10			5	10									5	10	5	10	
90	3	May	20	40 60	5	10					5	10			5	10									5	10	5	10	
90	3	Apr	20	40 60	5	10					5	10			5	10									5	10	5	10	
90	2	Mar	20	40 60	5	10					5	10			5	10									5	10	5	10	
90	2	Feb	20	40 60	5	10					5	10			5	10									5	10	5	10	
90	2	Jan	20	40 60	5	10					5	10			5	10									5	10	5	10	
90	1	Dec	20	40 60	5	10					5	10			5	10									5	10	5	10	
90	1	Nov	20	40 60	5	10					5	10			5	10									5	10	5	10	
89	4	Sep	20	40 60	10M 5F	20M 10F					5	10	5	10 GM4	5	10	5	10 GM4	5	10 GM4	5	10 GM4	5	10 GM4	5	10	5	10	
89	3	May	20	40 60	5	10					5	10		10	5	10									5	10	5	10	
88	3	May	20	40 60	5	10					5	10		10	5	10									5	10	5	10	
86	1	Dec	20	40 60	5	10	10	10		10	5	10			5	10									5	10	5	10	
83	1	Nov	15	30	10	20	5	10	5	10		10		10		10													

[1] Acronym Guide: A=mental category A, B=mental category B, C=currently enrolled in high school, F=female, G=high school graduate, H=non-high school graduate with GED or vocational/technical diploma, TSC IV, M=male, N=non-high graduate without GED or other diploma, P or PS=prior service, PPV=production point value (meeting goal), and OPV=overproduction point value. Blank spaces in the table indicate zeros.

[2] In the Success 2000 Program High School Graduates TSC I-IIIA = 30 points, High School Seniors TSC I-IIIA = 30 points, Other (Prior Service, Other High School Grad/Non Grad, No Gender/Mental Category) = 10 points

[3] In FY94 fourth quarter, the currently enrolled in high school (CA) category in the GSA and GSB columns was eliminated.

Appendix B

NAVY RECRUITING COMMAND COMPETITION SYSTEM FORMULAS FOR CALCULATING POINTS (Instruction 1650.8I FY89)

Enlisted NRCCS Annual Categories For FY89
(Points Awarded Based on FYTD Attainment)

Category	"Y"		Points Awarded
Total New Contract Objective	$\dfrac{\text{Total FYTD N/C Attained}}{\text{Total FYTD N/C Objective}}$	0 $60 + 1900\,(Y-1)$ 155	For Y<1.0 For $1.0 \le Y \le 1.05$ For Y > 1.05
NF New Contract Objective (Note 1)	$\dfrac{\text{NF FYTD N/C Attained}}{\text{NF FYTD N/C Objective}}$	$74\,(Y)^{15}$ $74 + 56.92\,(Y-1)^{0.5}$ 92	For Y<1.0 For $1.0 \le Y \le 1.1$ For Y > 1.1
NAM[a] UMG Accessions (Note 3)	$\dfrac{\text{NAM UMG Accessions}}{\text{NAM UMG Accession Goal}}$	0 54	For Y<1.0 For Y>1.0
Black UMG Accessions (Note 2)	$\dfrac{\text{Black UMG Accessions}}{\text{Black UMG Goal}}$	$104\,(Y)^{2}$ $104 + 50.84\,(Y-1)^{0.25}$ 138	For Y<1.0 For $1.0 \le Y \le 1.2$ For Y > 1.2
Hispanic UMG Accessions	$\dfrac{\text{Hispanic UMG Accessions}}{\text{Hispanic UMG Goal}}$	$66\,(Y)^{2}$ $66 + 35.89\,(Y-1)^{0.25}$ 90	For Y<1.0 For $1.0 \le Y \le 1.2$ For Y > 1.2

[a]Non-prior service active duty male.

Area and Districts Use the Same Formulas

Note 1: Points awarded only if FYTD NF accession goal is met.

Note 2: For area competition, bonus points are awarded only if UMG percentage targets (listed in comnavcruitcomnote 1133) are met. This does not apply to quarterly Admiral's Cup Competition.

Note 3: No points will be awarded in this category unless HSDG targets are also met.

Enlisted NRCCS Annual Categories For FY-89

Category	Points Awarded	
Active Duty (ACDU) Accession Goal	17	(Note 1)
DEP Management	8	(Note 2)
New Contract Objective	14	(Note 3)
NF Accessions	1	(Note 4)

Note 1: Active duty accession category includes the following programs: USN NPS, Male Active Mariner, Male TEP, USN NPS Female, Female Active Mariner, Female TEP, Total Prior Service and Total ACDU Accession Goals. Sixteen points will be awarded to each area or district that attains all program goals. A bonus of one fourth of one point will be awarded to each district for up to four overships; for areas, overship points will be awarded using a correction factor of $1/X$, where X is the number of districts in the area, up to a maximum of one point per month.

Note 2: DEP Management point are awarded based on the formulas below. To receive any points, the first out month's DEP percent must be at least 85%.

Part (A) DEP Profile

Adjusted DEP Profile Percent	=	1st Out Month DEP Percent	+	2nd Out Month DEP Percent	+	3rd Out Month DEP Percent	+	15%	−	In-Month Attrition Rollout Percent

Y = Adjusted DEP Profile Percent.

Points = 0	For $Y \leq 205$
$4 + [(Y-235)/7.5]$	For $205 < Y \leq 235$
4	For $Y > 235$

Part (B) In-Month Attrition and Rollout

Y = Adjusted DEP Profile Percent.

Points = 4	For $Y < 15$
$4 - 0.8 (Y-15)$	For $15 \leq Y \leq 20$
0	For $Y > 20$

Note 3: Monthly new contract points will be awarded in two subcategories as defined below:

(A)   Total new contracts

$$Y = (\text{NC Attainment}) / (\text{NC Objective})$$

$$\text{Points} = 7(Y)^8 \qquad \text{For } Y < 1.0$$

$$7 \qquad \text{For } Y \geq 1.0$$

(B)   Pivot Point New Contracts

Pivot Point New Contracts (PPNCs) are those written to ship between the present and the end of May, necessary to make shipping goal during that time frame. These contracts will be counted towards a Pivot Point Objective (PPO). Those contracts written into next June and beyond, regardless of whether they are will-graduate or work-force applicants do not count towards achievement of PPO.

The Pivot Point Percent (PP%) is the percent of the current month's NCO which must be PPNCs to ensure that accession goal will be attainable in the future. The PPO is the PP% expressed as a hard number goal for which the NRA/NRD will be held accountable. The PPO and PP% shall be determined as follows:

$$\text{PPO} = \text{Pivot Point Objective}$$

$$\text{PP\%} = \text{Pivot Point Percent}$$

$$\text{AG} = \text{Accession Goal (Present through May)}$$

$$\text{TD} = \text{Total DEP (Present through May)}$$

$$\text{NCOT} = \text{Total NCO (Present through May)}$$

$$\text{NCOP} = \text{Present Month's NCO}$$

$$\text{AF} = \text{Adjustment Factor} = 10.5\%$$

$$\text{PP\%} = 100(\text{AG} - \text{TD}) / (\text{NCOT}) \div (\text{AF})$$

$$\text{PPO} = (\text{PP\%}) (\text{NCOP})$$

*AF will be zero in the month of May.

$$Z = (\text{Pivot Point NC Attainment}) / (\text{PPO})$$

$$\text{Points} = 7(Z)^8 \qquad \text{For } Z < 1.0$$

$$7 \qquad \text{For } Z \geq 1.0$$

The total points earned for monthly new contracts will be the sum of the points earned in sub-categories (A) and (B).

Note 4: Nuclear Field Accession Overship Points are Awarded as Follows:

In March, April and May only:

NRD Points = 0.5 points per overship, limit one bonus point

NRA Points = (Area Overships) / (2 × number of NRDS), Limit one
bonus point

Enlisted Quarterly Award Categories For FY89

The enlisted quarterly award (Neptune's Cup) is intended to
stimulate increased competition by means of a shorter award period and
an award which is tied solely to enlisted production volume and good DEP
management. Constraints on this award are (1) that it may only be won
once in a fiscal year by any given NRD and (2) that any NRD that fails
to attain its Pivot Point Objective for any month during the quarter
will be eliminated from contention.

Category	Points Awarded
New contract objective	36 (Note 1)
DEP management	8 (Note 2)

Note 1: The quarterly new contract category will be treated like the
annual new contract category, insofar as points will be tracked
as though an entire quarter had been completed. To determine
actual points, multiply by a correction factor of X/3, where X
is 1, 2 or 3, depending on the number of months elapsed in the
quarter.

$$Y = \frac{\text{Total No. Attained for the Quarter}}{\text{Total NC Objective for the Quarter}}$$

Points = 24(Y)8   For Y < 1.0

36 - 12(Y)-8   For Y ≥ 1.0

Note 2: The DEP management points earned each month during the quarter
will be the same as the monthly category in the annual
completion (see above).

Appendix C

NAVY RECRUITING COMMAND RECRUITER ADVANCEMENT THROUGH EXCELLENCE (RATE) PROMOTION FORMULA TABLES FOR DISTRICTS AND ZONES (Instruction 1430.2--FY93)

District-Level Formulas for the Number of Promotion-Eligible Recruiters (September 1992 criteria)

Variable	Calculation
District Goal Achievement (DGA)	(% new contract achieved + % male "A" cell achieved) / 2^a
100% DGA < 106%	
% promotable	DGA - 100
# promotion-eligible	(% promotable / 100) X (# personnel on board)
DGA 106%	
% promotable	$6 + 952.2 \ [(DGA - 100) / 100]^{3.3559}$
# promotion-eligible	(% promotable / 100) X (# zone personnel on board)

[a]Male "A" cell = upper mental group/high school graduate. Added to formula April 1992.

Zone-Level Formulas for the Number of Promotion-Eligible Recruiters (September 1992 criteria)

Variable	Calculation
Zone Goal Achievement (ZGA)	(% new contract achieved + % male "A" cell achieved) / 2^a
100% ≥ ZGA < 106%	
% promotable	0.52 (ZGA - 100)
# promotion-eligible	(% promotable / 100) X (# zone personnel on board)
ZGA ≥ 106%	
% promotable	$0.52 \ \{6 + 952.2 \ [(ZGA - 100) / 100]^{3.3559}\}$
# promotion eligible	(% promotable / 100) X (# zone personnel on board)

[a]Male "A" cell = upper mental group/high school graduate. Added to formula April 1992.

Appendix D

**NAVY RECRUITING COMMAND RECRUITER EXCELLENCE INCENTIVE PROGRAM (REIP)
PRODUCTION PROMOTION FORMULAS FOR DISTRICTS (Instruction 1430.4--FY94)**

A. % District Goal Achievement

= (% new contract goal attained + % upper mental group goal attained)
/ 2
(Goals are fair-share annual goals determined by using the lowest
original or revised goal. Final FY production day is the last day of
the FY.)

B. For production at least 100% but less than 106%

% promotable = % Goal Achievement - 100
# promotion-eligible = (% promotable/100) X (# personnel on board)
(For number of personnel on board, divide the sum of those on board
the last day of each month by 12.)

C. For greater than 105.999% production

% promotable = 6 + 952.2[(% achievement -100) / (100)]$^{3.3559}$
# promotion-eligible = (% promotable/100) X (# personnel on board)

Final production promotion calculation--based on production promotions
available on the last day of the fiscal year.

Authorized promotions = a X (b/c)
a = # of promotion-eligible district personnel
b = total national promotions available
c = total # of personnel eligible for promotion nationally

Appendix E

NAVY RECRUITING COMMAND INDIVIDUAL AND UNIT ANNUAL INCENTIVE AWARDS TABLES (Instruction 1650.16D--FY94)

COMNAVCRUITCOM Individual Unit Awards Table

	Honors Awards			
Title of Award	TROPHY	LETTER OF COMM	ROY WEEK	NOTES
1. Recruiting District of the Year (George L. Carlin Award)	X		X	
2. Recruiting District of the Year Runner-Up (Charles E. Lofgren Award)	X			
3. Officer Recruiting District of the Year	X			
4. Enlisted Recruiting District of the Year	X			
5. Overall Station of the Year (Admiral's Cup)	X		X	1
6. Small Station of the Year (Admiral's Cup)	X			1
7. Medium Station of the Year (Admiral's Cup)	X			1
8. Large Station of the Year (Admiral's Cup)	X			1
9. Most Improved District of the Year (Officer and Enlisted)	X			2
10. Best District in Minority Recruiting (Officer and Enlisted)	X			3
11. Most Improved LEADS District	X	X		4
12. Best LEADS District (Officer and Enlisted)	X	X		4

Notes

1. <u>Station of the Year (Admiral's Cup)</u>. Awards will be presented for the best small, medium, and large stations of the year based on overall performance and goal attainment for the fiscal year in all categories. Area Commanders should submit area nominees for each of the three categories. The overall winner will be determined from those nominations and will receive an additional award. Each member of the station team will receive a Navy Achievement Medal and the station will receive an engraved Admiral's Cup trophy in addition to ROY week attendance. The RINCs from the other two stations of the year will attend ROY week also.

2. <u>Most Improved District of the Year and Most Improved Districts in Officer and Enlisted Recruiting</u>. The Most Improved District of the Year award is presented to NAVCRUITDISTs which have made the greatest strides in growth, recruiting potential and overall managerial performance in enlisted, officer, and overall recruiting categories.

3. <u>Best Districts in Minority Recruiting</u>. Minority recruiting is one of the more challenging aspects of being a recruiter. To be successful, recruiters must have a degree of sensitivity, awareness, and tenacity. There are two awards for minority recruiting – Best District in Minority Officer Recruiting which will be based on production in black and Hispanic recruiting and Best District in Minority Enlisted Recruiting which will be based on production in Black recruiting only.

4. <u>Best LEADS District and Most Improved LEADS District.</u> Enlisted and Officer LEADS contribution to new contract objective, Enlisted and Officer NALTS conversion rates and overall managerial performance are the factors used to determine Best LEADS District. Most improvements in LEADS and NALTS productivity (comparison between past and current fiscal years) and Lead Tracking Center support for the recruiter should determine Most Improved LEADS District. Submission will be in standard letter format addressing the above criteria.

COMNAVCRUITCOMM Individual Awards Table

LEGEND

ROY - Recruiter of the Year
(AW) - Area Winner
(NW) - National Winner

Title	Eligibility Requirements	Honors Awards: MERITORIOUS ADV	NCM	NAM	LETTER OF COMM	TROPHY	ROY WEEK	NOTES
ENL ROY (AW)	All recruiters assigned to recruiting production and on production for at least 9 months of the competitive period			X			X	
OFF ROY (AW)	All officer recruiters assigned to COMNAVCRUITCOM field activities			X			X	
CHIEF ROY (AW)	All recruiters assigned as Chief Recruiter for at least nine months of the competitive period			X				
ENG ROY (AW)	All recruiters assigned to COMNAVCRUITCOM field activities			X				
MEDICAL ROY (AW)	All recruiters assigned to COMNAVCRUITCOM field activities			X				
NROTC ROY (AW)	All officially designated and functioning Navy Reserve Officer Training Corps/Broadened Opportunity for Officer Selection and Training (NROTC/BOOST) coordinates for the 12 consecutive months preceding nomination. (only military personnel are eligible for this award)			X				
ZONE SUP ROY (AW)	All recruiters assigned as Zone Supervisor for at least nine months of the competitive period			X				

COMNAVCRUITCOM Individual Awards Table

LEGEND

ROY - Recruiter of the Year
(AW) - Area Winner
(NW) - National Winner

Title	Eligibility Requirements	MERITORIOUS ADV	NCM	NAM	LETTER OF COMM	TROPHY	ROY WEEK	NOTES
ENL ROY (NW)	All recruiters assigned to recruiting production and on production for at least nine months of the competitive period	X	X			X	X	
OFF ROY (NW)	All officer recruiters assigned to COMNAVCRUITCOM field activities		X			X	X	1
CHIEF ROY (NW)	All recruiters assigned as Chief Recruiter for at least nine months of the competitive period		X			X	X	
ENG ROY (NW)	All recruiters assigned to COMNAVCRUITCOM field activities		X			X		1
MEDICAL ROY (NW)	All recruiters assigned to COMNAVCRUITCOM field activities		X			X		1
NROTC ROY (NW)	All officially designated and functioning NROTC/BOOST coordinates for the 12 consecutive months preceding nomination (only military personnel are eligible for this award)		X			X	X	
ZONE SUP ROY (NW)	All recruiters assigned as Zone Supervisor for at least nine months of the competitive period		X			X	X	
CLO OF YEAR (NW)	All CLOs in support of recruiting		X			X	X	2

Honors Awards

COMNAVCRUITCOM Individual Awards Table

		Honors Awards						
	LEGEND ROY - Recruiter of the Year (AW) - Area Winner (NW) - National Winner	M E R I T O R I O U S A D V	N C M	N A M	L E T T E R O F C O M M	T R O P H Y	R O Y W E E K	N O T E S
Title	Eligibility Requirements							
EDSPEC (NW)	All civilian billet incumbents who have filled the position at least one year as of 31 August of the current year				X	X	X	3
CLASSIFIER OF THE YEAR	All classifiers who have functioned as a classifier for at least nine months of the competitive period		X			X	X	
RDAC OF THE YEAR	All civilian, reservists, or retired personnel who are serving or have served as Chairperson of RDAC during the competitive period		X			X	X	4
NUC FLD ROY	All Nuclear Field Recruiters who have functioned as such for at least nine months of the competitive period		X			X	X	
SUPPORT PERSON	All billet incumbents who have functioned as such for at least nine months during the fiscal year (military and civilian personnel are eligible)		X			X	X	
LEAD TRACKING CENTER SUPERVISOR	All LEAD Tracking Center Supervisors who have functioned as such for at least nine months of the competitive period		X			X	X	

Appendix F

AIR FORCE RECRUITING SERVICE COMPETITION SYSTEM FY87 TO FY93; FY95

Table F.1[1]
Air Force Recruiting Service Competition System
FY87 to FY93; FY95

Categories	FY87 Points	FY88 Points	FY89 Points	FY90 Points	FY91 Points	FY92 Points	FY93 Points	FY95 Points
Enlisted Programs								
Non-prior-service accessions[2]	15.75	12.5	15	19	14	5	16	10
Non-prior-service accessions mental category I[3]				3	3		1	10
Non-prior-service contracts	15.75	12.5	16	20	13	15	16	10
Prior service accessions[4]	3.5		2	1				
Officer Training School (OTS) programs[5]	8.25	3.4			2	2	2	
Black officer training school applications						2		1
Minority officer training school applications							3	3
Hispanic ROTC								1
ROTC[6]					1 (+1)	1		1
Black ROTC		5	5	1	2 (+1)	2 (+1)	3	1
ROTC scholarship applications					1	1	1	
Student vocational aptitude tests administered[7]	5	5	1	2	1	2		
Non-scholarships referrals		5	3					
Eligible scholarship programs					4			
Combat controllers/parachute jumpers								1
Basic military training attrition – male								3
Basic military training attrition – female								1
Ship day cancellations								2
Health Professions								
Physicians[8]	21	20	17	16	15	25	20	12
Physician specialist				3	3			Vary by Type
Nurses[9]	16	15.5	17	16	18	12	12	10
Nurse specialist[10]				3	3	4		Vary by Type
Allied health[11]	5.5	6.75		5	5	2		
Health professions scholarship program[12]			2				1	1
Medical service corps			2				0.3	2
Dentist			2				1.5	3
Biomedical sciences (BSC)	7.5	7.75	9	8	12	22	6	2
PA/PT[13]							6	

Table F.1 (Continued)

Categories	FY87 Points	FY88 Points	FY89 Points	FY90 Points	FY91 Points	FY92 Points	FY93 Points	FY95 Points
Officer Programs								
Navigator	1.75	3.3	2					
Non-rated operations		3.3	2					
Technical								
Non-technical			1					
Pilot			2					
Allied[14]				2				
Commander emphasis[15]								
Minority officer training accessions[16]								
PT/PT						5		
Mental category I accessions				2			2	
Flight Success[17]							5	
Operation ASAP - FY 92[18]								
Activity Watch '92[19]								
Mechanical GTEP or AIS[20]								
Black officer training applications[21]								
Total Points[22]	100	100	100	98	96	100	100	
Bonus points[23]								
>100% in non-ATB			3% of total points					
Physician			5% of total points					
Nurse specialist			5% of total points					
ROTC nurse scholarship applications			2% of total points					

NOTES:

[1] Source: Fiscal year annual written announcements from Air Force Recruiting Service to groups and squadrons.

[2] In FY90, NPS accessions points were deleted from competition because the DEP was too low.

[3] This program was added for one year and was not goaled. In FY90 and FY93, it was a Commander's Emphasis Program.

[4] In FY88, prior-service accessions were added to net contracts.

[5] In FY93, points applied to Applications Program only.

[6] In FY90, must achieve black subgoal and overall goal to receive points. In FY91, a Phase I ROTC subset awarded 1 additional point each for black and total applications between June and October 15. In FY92, in a Phase I subset, 1 point was awarded for black applications.

[7] Students who take the Armed Services Vocational Aptitude Battery (ASVAB) tests in a school or training institution.

[8] In FY91, total physician program = 15 points, fully qualified = 6 points, and level 2 program = credit towards goaled program.

[9] In FY90 and FY92, double points were awarded for Certified Registered Nurse Anesthetist (CRNA), and Health Program Scholarship Program (HPSP) Nurse Anesthetist commissions.

[10] In FY91, double credit was awarded in the Nurse Specialist Program.

[11] In all years except FY89 and FY93, dentists, Medical Service Corps (MSC), and Health Program Scholarship Programs were in Allied Health. In FY89, 2 points were awarded individually to the three categories. In FY93, dentists received 1.5 points (.75 without achieving goal), and Health Program Scholarships received 1 point.

[12] In FY91, minorities were awarded double credit.

[13] In FY93, PA/PTs were awarded 6 points for the first contract, 3 points for the second, and 1 point for each additional PA/PT in a program separate from BSC.

[14] Navigator, non-rated operations, pilot, pilot technical.

[15] See text for description.

[16] OTS accessions earned double credit in FY88 for minorities and in FY89 and FY91 for blacks.

[17] FY93 - a flight contract goal program based on monthly and annual goal attainment, with 5 points for achieving goal. The squadron formula was (# of successful Flights/ # of Flights X 13) X 5. (13 =1yr & 12 months).

[18] See text for description. Awarded prizes, not points e.g., watches to all meeting criteria, grand prize=3-day trip.

[19] See text for description. Awarded prizes not points for accessions, e.g., watches to 10 recruiters and 3 to Supervisor/group.

[20] See text for description.

[21] Applications in this category count towards the OTS Application Program category. In FY90, double points were awarded.

[22] FY91 can be greater than 100 because extra ROTC bonus points were awarded. FY93 does not add to 100 because a sliding scale was used in some programs.

[23] Points awarded as specified for achieving 100 percent of goal or greater in non-ATB programs.

Appendix G

AIR FORCE RECRUITING SERVICE INCENTIVE AWARDS PROGRAM

Table G.1

Air Force Recruiting Service Incentive Awards Program
(Recruiting Groups)
FY90 To FY95

Award Category/Program	Effective Date	Award Criteria[1]	Award[2]
Top Overall	Aug. 90 – Feb. 92	Highest point score in competition system	Rotating bowl
	Mar. 92 – Nov. 94	Highest point score in competition system and goal met in emphasis programs[3]	Rotating bowl & permanent plaque
Top Enlisted program	Aug. 90 – Feb. 92	Achieves 100% of goal and highest enlisted program score in competition system	Plaque
	Mar. 92 – Nov. 94	Achieves enlisted program goal with highest total enlisted program score in competition system, and achieves assigned goals in contracts, accessions, students tested, ROTC, ROTC black, OTS, and OTS minority applications[4]	Plaque
	Dec. 94 to present	Selected by Headquarters based on production, special emphasis or non-goaled program, achievement, and other discretionary performance quality elements.	Plaque
Top OTS program	Aug. 90 – Feb. 91	Achieves 100% of goal and highest OTS program score in competition system	Plaque
Top Physician Program	Aug. 90 – Feb. 92	Achieves 100% of goal and highest physician program score in competition system	Plaque

Table G.1 (continued)

Award Category/Program	Effective Date	Award Criteria	Award
	Mar. 92 – Jan. 93	Achieves physician program goal with highest physician program score in competition system	Plaque
Top Medical[5]	Aug. 90 – Feb. 92	Achieves 100% of goal and highest total BSC and allied health program score in competition system	Plaque
Top BSC and AH[6]	Mar. 92 – Jan. 93	Achieves BSC and AH program goals with highest total program score + goal in BSC & AH. Makes 2 of 3 individual AH program goals & total AH program goal	Plaque
Top Medical[7]	Feb. 93 – Nov. 94	Achieves all medical programs goals with highest medical program score. Includes MSC, PA, PT	Plaque
Top Medical	Dec. 94 to present	Selected by Headquarters based on production, special emphasis or non-goaled program, achievement, and other discretionary performance quality elements.	Plaque
Top Nurse program (nurse and nurse specialist)	Aug. 90 – Feb. 92	Achieves 100% of goal and highest nurse program score in competition system	Plaque
	Mar. 92 – Nov. 94	Achieves nurse program goal with highest nurse program score in competition system	Plaque

Table G.1 (continued)

Award Category/Program	Effective Date	Award Criteria	Award
	Dec. 94 to present	Selected by Headquarters based on production, special emphasis or non-goaled program, achievement, and other discretionary performance quality elements.	Plaque
Top Health Professions Team	Aug. 90 -Nov.94	Achieves health profession goal with highest program score and goal	Plaque
	Dec. 94 - present	Selected by headquarters based on production, special emphasis or non-goaled program, achievement, and other discretionary performance quality elements.	Plaque
Top ASVAB[8]	Aug. 90 - Feb. 91	Highest percentage ASVAB goal achieved for high school juniors and seniors tested	Trophy or plaque
	Mar. 91 - Nov. 94	Highest ASVAB program score and ASVAB goal achieved	Plaque
Top Safety program	Aug. 90 - Feb. 92	Criteria not available	Plaque
	Mar. 92 to present	Top FY safety program	Plaque
ATB[9]	Aug. 90 - Feb. 92	Achieves 100% of goal in all goaled programs	Plaque to each achieving group
Mission Accomplishment[10]	Mar. 92 to present	Achieves all assigned goals	Plaque
Annual Standard Of Excellence[11]			

Table G.1 (continued)

Award Category/Program	Effective Date	Award Criteria	Award
Enlisted/non-prior-service contracts and accessions	Aug. 90 – Feb. 92	Achieve 100% of goal in contracts and accessions. Total goals in all programs must be greater than 115% achievement and all ASVAB goal achievements must be 100%	Plaque to each achieving group
	Mar. 92 to Nov. 94	Makes goal in non-prior-service contracts and accessions, student ASVAB, total ROTC and ROTC black applications. OTS application programs, and all enlisted contracts written must be 115% of total goal or greater.	Plaque
	Dec. 94 to present	Makes goal in non-prior-service contracts and accessions, total ROTC and ROTC minority applications, OTS applications programs, and OTS minority applications. All enlisted contracts written must be 115% of total goal or greater.	
OTS	Aug. 90 – Feb. 91	Achieve 100% of goal in all assigned OTS goals and the cumulative total of all goals must be ≥115%	Plaque to each achieving group
Medical	Aug. 90 – Feb. 92	Achieve 100% of goal in all assigned medical goals + cumulative total of all goals must be 115% except physician	Plaque to each achieving group
BSC and AH	Mar. 92 – Jan 93	Achieves goal in BSC and AH program. Make 2 of 3 AH program goals & total AH program. BSC contracts must be 115% of goal	Plaque to each achieving group

Table G.1 (continued)

Award Category/Program	Effective Date	Award Criteria	Award
Medical	Feb. 93 - Nov. 94	Achieve goal in all medical programs and all contracts written must be 115% of goal	Plaque to each achieving group
Nurse (and nurse specialist)	Aug. 90 - Feb. 92	Achieve 100% of goal in overall assigned nurse goals & the cumulative total of all goals must be 115%	Plaque to each achieving group
	Mar. 92 to Nov. 94	Achieve goal in nurse program and the cumulative total of all nurse contracts must be 115%[12]	
Monthly contracts	Feb. 93 - Mar. 94	Achieve 115% of monthly total contracts written goal	Plaque to each achieving group
Physician	Aug. 90 - Jan 93	Achieve 100% of physician goal	Plaque to each achieving group

Information for this table was obtained from the Recruiting Service Incentive Awards Program ATC Regulation 900-18 issued August 24, 1990, March 18, 1991, March 27, 1992, February 23, 1993, and from Recruiting Service Incentive Awards Program AETC Instruction 36-2804, December 15, 1994. The Awards Program is an annual program measuring from one FY to the next FY. Regulations, however, are re-issued only when they are revised. Information in this table is displayed in conformance with changes in the regulation.

[1]In general, when a criterion specifies achieving a goal and achieving a program goal, some but not all of the program's components are goaled in addition to a total program goal. For example, the Annual Standard of Excellence enlisted category for March 1992 to November 1994 specifies goaled components requiring 100 percent achievement in addition to 115 percent or greater achievement for the entire program goal.

[2]Competition System awards in this table are all those with criteria requiring highest rank in the Competition System or highest program score. These are Top Overall, Top Enlisted, Top OTS, Top Physician, Top Medical, Top Nurse, Top Health Professions Team, and Top ASVAB.

[3]Emphasis programs are the most important to achieve. They may or may not be designated annually, depending on need. In FY89, the emphasis programs were contracts, accessions, physicians, BSC, and nurses. In FY95, there were no emphasis programs. (Based on HQAFRS interview, no documentation.)

[4]All listed programs may not be in the enlisted program goal.

[5]This program changed names and components over the years. See footnotes 6 and 7 for details.

[6]Biomedical Science Corps includes all licensed health professionals. Allied Health from 8/90 to 1/93 included the dental program, Medical Service Corps program, and Health Professions Schooling programs. No information for February 1993 on.

[7]Medical combines physician, Biomedical Sciences Corps and Allied Health.

[8]This program measures the number of people tested for vocational ability and potential placement.

[9]The term ATB is used to signify that 100 percent of all goals either overall or in a program are achieved.

[10]Name changed from ATB to Mission Accomplishment. The table lists Mission Accomplishment to conform with the change, although the more common term ATB is used throughout the report.

[11]Annual Standard of Excellence awards are given to all units that satisfy the criteria. Excellence as defined by the criteria rather than highest achievement is rewarded.

[12]All nurse contracts includes nurse specialist, nurse scholarships, etc.

- 89 -

Table G.2

Air Force Recruiting Service Incentive Awards Program
Recruiting Squadrons
FY90 to FY 95

Award Category/Program	Effective Date	Award Criteria[1]	Award[2]
Top Squadron	Aug. 90 - Feb. 92	Highest rank in competition system	Plaque
	Mar. 92 - Nov. 94	Highest rank in competition system, and goal met in emphasis program[3]	Plaque
	Dec. 94 to present	One award for each squadron by overall quality contribution to Air Force[4]	Plaque
Most Improved	Aug. 90 to present	Nominated by group commander, no specific criteria	Plaque
Recruiting Service Quality	Feb. 93 to present	Best implementation of Quality Air Force (QAF), significant improvements, high quality service[5]	Plaque
Advertising and Promotion (A&P) Program[6]	Mar. 92 to present	Annual guidelines	Plaque
Top Public Service Programs	Aug. 90 - Feb. 92	Highest program score based on narrative written to nominate a squadron	Plaque
Top Safety Programs	Aug. 90 to present	Criteria not available	Plaque
Top ASVAB tests administered[7]	Aug. 90 - Feb. 92	Highest percentage ASVAB goal achieved for high school juniors and seniors tested	Trophy or plaque

Table G.2 (continued)

Award Category/Program	Effective Date	Award Criteria	Award
	Mar. 92 - Nov. 94	Highest student ASVAB program score and achievement of ASVAB goal	Trophy or plaque
Top BSC and AH[8]	Mar. 92 - Jan. 93	Achieves BSC and AH program goals with highest total program score. Make 2 of 3 individual AH program goals & total AH program goal	Plaque
Top Health Professions Team	Aug. 90 - Nov. 94	Achieves 100% of goal in all assigned health profession goals and highest health professions score in competition system	Rotating trophy and permanent plaque
	Dec. 94 to present	By nomination - no criteria specified	Plaque
Top Medical Team	Mar. 91 - Nov. 94	Achieves 100% of goal in all assigned medical goals and achieves highest medical competition system score	Plaque
	Dec. 94 to present	By nomination - no criteria specified	Plaque
Top Nurse Team (Nurse & Nurse Specialist)	Mar. 91 - Nov. 94	Achieves 100% of goal in overall assigned nurse goal and achieves highest score in competition system	Plaque
	Dec. 94 to present	By nomination - no criteria specified	Plaque
Top Physician Team	Mar. 92 - Jan. 93	Achieves goal in physician program with highest physician program score in the competition system	Plaque
ATB	Aug. 90 - Feb. 92	Achieves 100% of all goaled programs	

Table G.2 (continued)

Award Category/Program	Effective Date	Award Criteria	Award
Mission Accomplishment[9]	Mar. 92 - present	Achieves all assigned goals	Plaque to each achieving squadron
Facilities Enhancement Award	Feb. 93 to present	Annual guidelines from Headquarters Recruiting Service Logistics/Information Management	Plaque
Top Recruiting Service MEPS	Mar. 91 - Feb. 92	Top MEPS score in Competition System	Plaque to MEPS and each LNCO
	Mar 92 - Nov. 94	Highest effectiveness rate in Competition System[10]	Plaque to MEPS and each LNCO
	Dec. 94 to present	By nomination - no criteria specified	Plaque to MEPS and each LNCO[11]
MEPS Procedural Excellence	Aug. 90 - Feb. 91	Full error-free FY	Plaque
Annual Standard of Excellence[12]			
Enlisted/Non-Prior-Service Contracts and Accessions	Aug. 90 - Feb. 92	Achieves 100% of all goals in contracts and accessions. Total goals in all programs must be ≥115%, and all ASVAB goals must be 100%	Plaque - each achieving squadron
	Mar. 92 - Nov. 94	Makes goal in non-prior-service contracts and accessions, student ASVAB, total ROTC and ROTC black applications, OTS application programs; all enlisted contracts written must be ≥115% of goal	Plaque - each achieving squadron

Table G.2 (continued)

Award Category/Program	Effective Date	Award Criteria	Award
	Dec. 94 to present	Makes goal in non-prior-service contracts and accessions, total ROTC and ROTC minority applications, OTS applications programs, and OTS minority applications. All enlisted contracts written must be ≥115% of goal	Plaque – each achieving squadron
OTS	Aug. 90 – Feb. 91	Achieves 100% of goal in all assigned OTS goals and the cumulative total of all goals must be ≥115%	Plaque – each achieving squadron
Medical	Aug. 90 – Feb. 92	Achieves 100% of goal in all assigned medical goals + cumulative total of all goals must be ≥115% except Physician	Plaque – each achieving squadron
BSC and AH	Mar. 92 – Jan. 93	Achieves goal BSC and AH program. Make 2 of 3 AH program goals & total AH program. BSC contracts goal must be ≥ 115%	Plaque – each achieving squadron
Medical	Feb. 93 to Nov. 94	Achieve goal in all medical programs and total contracts written must be ≥115% of goal	Plaque – each achieving squadron
Nurse	Aug. 90 – Jan. 93	Achieves 100% of goal in overall assigned nurse goals & the cumulative total of all goals must be ≥115%	Plaque – each achieving squadron
Physician	Aug. 90 – Jan 93	100% of physician goal or more	Plaque – each achieving squadron

Table G.2 (continued)

Award Category/Program	Effective Date	Award Criteria	Award
Monthly for contracts	Feb. 93 - Nov. 94	Achieves ≥115% monthly total contracts written goal	Plaque - each achieving squadron Awarded Monthly
MEPS operations	Aug. 90 - Feb. 91	Top 5 Competition System scorers each in small, medium, and large MEPS	Plaque - each achieving MEPS
	Mar. 91 - Feb. 92	70 points in Competition System or FY error free	Plaque - each achieving MEPS
	Mar. 92 - Nov. 94	Top seven MEPS in Competition System based on effectiveness rate	Plaque - each achieving MEPS

Information for this table was obtained from the Recruiting Service Incentive Awards Program Regulation 900-18 issued August 24, 1990, March 18, 1991, March 27, 1992, February 23, 1993, and from Recruiting Service Incentive Awards Program, AETC Instruction 36-2804, December 15, 1994. The Awards Program is an annual program measuring from one FY to the next FY. Regulations, however, are re-issued only when they are revised. Information in this table is displayed in conformance with changes in the regulation.

1In general, when a criterion specifies achieving a goal and achieving a program goal, some but not all program components are goaled in addition to a total program goal. For example, the Annual Standard of Excellence enlisted category for March 1992 to November 1994 specifies goaled components requiring 100 percent achievement in addition to 115 percent or greater achievement for the entire program goal.
2Competition System awards in this table are all those with criteria requiring highest rank in the Competition System or highest program score. These are Top Squadron, Top Enlisted, Top OTS, Top Physician, Top Medical, Top Nurse, Top ASVAB, Top BSC and AH, Top ASVAB Tests Administered, Top Health Professions Team, Top Medical Team, Top Nurse Team, Top Medical Team, Top MEPS, and Top MEPS Operations.

[3] Emphasis programs are the most important to achieve. They may or may not be designated annually, depending on need. In FY89, the emphasis programs were contracts, accessions, physicians, BSC, and nurses. In FY95, there were no emphasis programs. (Based on HQAFRS interview, no documentation.)

[4] Quality refers to squadron management quality.

[5] Quality Air Force (QAF) is a squadron management program.

[6] All public service message time or space in electronic or in printed form is donated. From August 1990 to February 1992, to encourage recruiters to obtain donations, the Advertising and Program Division conducted a program with points for recruiter achievement competition. Points were awarded for number of donated public service minutes, billboards, newspaper ads, etc., donated.

[7] This program measures the number of people tested for vocational ability and potential placement in the Air Force.

[8] Biomedical Science Corps includes all licensed health professionals. Allied Health from 8/90 to 1/93 included the dental program, Medical Service Corps program, and Health Professions Schooling programs. No information for February 1993 on.

[9] Name changed from ATB to Mission Accomplishment. The table lists Mission Accomplishment to conform with the change, although the more common term ATB is used throughout the report.

[10] Effectiveness rate is the total number of recruits reporting to the MEPS for processing minus the total number who report for duty.

[11] LNCO stands for Liaison Non-commissioned Officer. These are the MEPS job counselors.

[12] Annual Standard of Excellence awards are given to all units that satisfy the criteria. Excellence as defined by the criteria rather than highest achievement is rewarded.

Table G.3

Air Force Recruiting Service Incentive Awards Program

Individuals

FY90 to FY95

Award Category/Program	Regulation Date	Award Criteria[1]	Award[2]
Top Flight Supervisor	Aug. 90 – Feb. 92	Must be 100% or more in all goaled programs. Nomination justified by flight goal and accession achievement, marketing activities, awards received, and safety compliance and initiatives.	Trophy or plaque
	Mar. 92 to present	Flight achieves all assigned goals. Supervisor in production position for full FY[3]	Plaque
Top Health Professions Flight Supervisor	Mar. 91 – present	Must be 100% or more in all goaled programs. Flight achieves all assigned goals. Supervisor in production position for full FY	Plaque
Top Recruiter	Aug. 90 – Feb. 92	Must be 100% or more in all goaled programs assigned. Selected from Top Physician, Medical, Nurse, OTS, and Enlisted Programs winners	Trophy or plaque
	Mar. 92 – Jan. 93	Selected from Top Enlisted, Top Physician, BSC & AH, and Nurse winners	Plaque
	Feb. 93 to present	Selected from Top Enlisted, Medical, and Nurse winners	Plaque

Table G.3 (continued)

Award Category/Program	Regulation Date	Award Criteria	Award
Top OTS Recruiter	Aug. 90 – Feb. 91	Nominee must have been assigned individual Net Select goals[4]	Trophy or plaque
Top Rookie Recruiter	Aug. 90 – Feb. 92	Must be 100% or more in all goals assigned. Must be achieved during the first 12 months on duty as a recruiter	Trophy or plaque
	Mar. 92 – Nov. 94	Must achieve all assigned goals during the first 12 months on duty as a recruiter	Plaque
	Dec. 94 – present	Must be Senior Recruiter Badge recipient during initial 12 months as a recruiter[5]	Plaque
Top Enlisted Programs Recruiter	Aug. 90 – Feb. 92	Production nominee who is ≥100% in all assigned goaled programs, and is a recruiter for a full FY (except Rookie Recruiter)	Trophy or plaque
	Mar. 92 to present	Achieves all assigned goals and is a recruiter for a full FY	Plaque
Top Physician Recruiter	Aug. 90 – Feb. 92	Achieves all assigned goals and is assigned individual accession goals	Trophy or plaque
	Mar. 92 – Jan. 93	Achieves all assigned goals, is assigned individual accession goals and is a recruiter for a full FY	Plaque
Top Medical Recruiter[6]	Aug. 90 – Feb. 92	Achieves all assigned goals and is assigned individual accession goals	Trophy or plaque

Table G.3 (continued)

Award Category/Program	Regulation Date	Award Criteria	Award
Top BSC and AH[7] Recruiter	Mar. 92 – Jan. 93	Achieves all assigned goals, is assigned individual accession goal, and is a recruiter for a full FY	Plaque
Top Medical Recruiter[8]	Feb. 93 – Nov. 94	Achieves all assigned goals or team achieves 100% of goal	Plaque
	Dec. 94 to present	Achieves all assigned goals and accession goal, or team achieves 100% of goal	Plaque
Top Nurse Recruiter	Aug. 90 – Feb. 92	Achieves all assigned goals and is assigned individual accession goals	Trophy or plaque
	Mar. 92 – Jan. 93	Achieves all assigned goals, is assigned individual accession goal, and is a recruiter for a full FY	Plaque
	Feb. 93 to present	Achieves all assigned goals and accession goal, or team achieves 100% of goal	Plaque
Top MEPS NCO	Aug. 90 – Feb. 92	Not specified. Nomination justification includes support of unit and recruiters, rapport with commanders, processing innovations, civilian awards, community activities, continuing education levels, squadron and group awards, and safety	Trophy or plaque

Table G.3 (continued)

Award Category/Program	Regulation Date	Award Criteria	Award
	Mar. 92 to Nov. 94	Not specified. Nomination justification includes accomplishments, continuing education level, rapport with commanders, community activities, and safety	Plaque
	Dec. 94 to present	Not specified. Nomination justification includes job and other accomplishments	
Top Support NCO	Aug. 90 – Feb. 92	Not specified. Nomination justification includes FY duty accomplishment, squadron/base activities, civilian awards, community activities, continuing education levels, squadron and group awards, and safety	Trophy or plaque
	Mar. 92 to Jan. 93	Not specified. Nomination justification includes job and other accomplishments, community activities, continuing education level, squadron/base activities, safety	Plaque
Top 99500 Support NCO[9]	Aug. 90 – Feb. 92	Not specified. Nomination justification includes FY duty accomplishment, support of flights/recruiters, squadron/base activities, civilian awards, community activities, continuing education levels, squadron and group awards, and safety	Trophy or plaque

Table G.3 (continued)

Award Category/Program	Regulation Date	Award Criteria	Award
	Mar. 92 – Nov. 94	Not specified. Nomination justification includes job and other accomplishments, community activities, continuing education level, squadron/base activities, safety	Plaque
Top 8R000 Support NCO	Dec. 94 to present	Not specified. Nomination justification includes job and other accomplishments	Plaque
Top Civilian	Aug. 90 – Feb. 92	Not specified. Nomination justification includes job accomplishment, support of flights/recruiters, innovations, group/squadron awards, community activities, and safety	Trophy or plaque
	Mar. 92 to present	Not specified. Nomination justification includes job and other accomplishment	Plaque
Top Group Safety Program Manager	Aug. 90 – Feb. 91	Not specified	Trophy or plaque
Operation Blue Suit	Aug. 90 – Jan. 93	Annual criteria from recruiting commander	Announced annually by recruiting commander
	Feb. 93 to present	Annual criteria from recruiting commander	Shadowbox
Spouse of the Year	Feb. 93 to present	Participates or contributes to initiatives/activities impacting RS, and/or AF mission (nomination)	Plaque

Table G.3 (continued)

Award Category/Program	Regulation Date	Award Criteria	Award
Langley Spirit Award	Feb. 93 to present	Spirit, enthusiasm, and determination to accomplish mission	Plaque
Master and Senior Recruiting Badge	Aug. 90 to present	(See text for description)	(See text for description)

Information for this table was obtained from the Recruiting Service Incentive Awards Program Regulation 900-18 issued August 24, 1990, March 18, 1991, March 27, 1992, February 23, 1993, and from Recruiting Service Incentive Awards Program, AETC Instruction 36-2804, December 15, 1994. The Awards Program is an annual program measuring from one FY to the next FY. Regulations, however, are only re-issued when they are revised. Information in this table is displayed in conformance with changes in the regulation.

[1] Criteria are primary criteria for each program or category. Awards Program regulations sometimes contain more detailed specifications. Additionally, when criteria were not specified or vague (primarily from August 1990 to February 1992), topics specified in the justification section of the award nomination form are listed.
[2] Award winners in the following categories receive their awards and are recognized at the annual Recruiting Service Commander Conference Awards Banquet. August 1990 to February 1991 included winners of individual achievement awards, senior liaison non-commissioned officer of Top MEPS, and Top Health Professions Team managers. March 1991 to February 1993 included all of the above and Top Medical Team managers and Top Nurse Program Team managers. March 1992 to November 1994 included all the above and Gold Medal Olympiad winners. Conference attendees not listed after December 1994.
[3] The term production is used to refer to producing to achieve a goal. This means any goal by a unit or individual in any program or category.
[4] Net Select is the number of recruits selected to attend OTS minus the number that do not report to OTS.
[5] See text for description of Senior Recruiter Badge.
[6] This program changed name and components over the years. See footnotes 8 and 9 for details.
[7] Biomedical Science Corps includes all licensed health professionals. Allied Health from 8/90 to 1/93 included the dental program, Medical Service Corps program, and Health Professions Schooling programs. No information for February 1993 on.
[8] Medical combines Physician, Biomedical Sciences Corps, and Allied Health.
[9] 99500 and 8R000 are designations used to mean any enlisted recruiter.

Appendix H

AIR FORCE ONE-TIME INCENTIVE PROGRAMS

Activity Watch '92 was implemented in response to a national mid-year call for 5500 additional non-prior-service accessions with a particular requirement to speedily process high school graduates. All new applicants who signed contracts during the four-month competition period were counted toward a recruiter's award total. To meet the immediate need, high school graduates booked and processed during the first two competition months were credited as two recruits. Recruiters and flight supervisors were eligible. Since the size of flights can vary, flight supervisor accomplishment was measured as an average of flight production. Winners received watches, presented by the commander if he was available, and documented recognition at Headquarters and in the recruiter magazine.

Operation ASAP was a six-month special emphasis program instituted in 1992 by the Commander to increase activity in health profession programs. Operation ASAP meant Actively Seeking Another Provider, specifically in the physician, physician assistant, and physical therapist categories. All applications received at the recruiting squadron after the program inception date were counted. For award consideration, individual recruiters needed to submit at least one new application in each category. When teams competed, one contract per recruiter was required. All recruiters writing two or more contracts in one category received a wristwatch. The top three recruiters in each category received a three-day expense- and duty-free vacation. Additionally, squadrons with three or more contracts (one or more for groups) in either category were awarded a wildcard enlistment to apply to any allied health or nurse specialist program goal. Squadrons or groups that satisfied both the physician and PA/PT requirements received two wildcard enlistments they could apply to their nurse program or allied health program goals.

Mechanical GTEP or AI was a FY95 national incentive program to increase the number of Mechanical GTEP or AI recruits. Mechanical GTEP is a Guaranteed Training Enlistment Program for jet engine mechanics, and AI is an applicant's aptitude index (in this case for mechanics). A recruiter was required to achieve his or her assigned contract goal between November 1, 1994, and February 28, 1995. Those satisfying the goal were eligible to receive one point for each mechanic career field reservation during the four-month time frame; they lost one point for each cancellation. Nine accrued points were required to compete in this incentive program. All eligible recruiters received a recruiting service portfolio-calendar and the opportunity to become a group winner. Winners who achieved the highest point total in their group received a flight in a T-37 or T-38 at Randolph Air Force Base, dinner with the Commander, a plaque, and other recruiting service gifts.

Appendix I

MARINE CORPS DISTRICT INCENTIVE PLANS (EXAMPLES)

1ST DISTRICT

Three district plans covering the 1990s vary in the participants included, emphasis, and measurement schemes. In most years, district winners and one winner per recruiting station were recognized. The following are brief summaries of the three plans.

FY91. In FY91, recruiting stations, recruiting sub-stations, NCOICs, and recruiters participated in the district program. Recruiting unit awards were issued by the district commander and presented to recruiting units by the district commander. Individual awards were presented at lower levels by recruiting station commanders, and at higher levels by district commanders.

Recruiting stations competed at the district level in overall performance for monthly, quarterly, and annual awards based on an established point system, and quarterly for recruiting unit quality, operating standards, attrition rates, disqualifications, etc. Points were awarded as a percentage of achievement for some categories (shipping, contracts, phaseline, and other categories), or as designated points for others (i.e., unit operating standards including failures, administration, and others.[1] For example, the category "achieving or exceeding shipping mission" was worth 10 points. If a recruiting station achieved 104 percent, the total point calculation was:

$$1.04 \times 10 = 10.4 \text{ total shipping points}$$

Unit quality categories were worth 0.5 to 3 points for achieving set standards.

The awards included trophies, plaques, medals, certificates, and cups.

---

[1]Phaseline is a recruiting period, normally one week. Some units set phaseline goals.

FY94. The FY94 plan reduced the number of recruiting station awards by 60 percent (from 5 to 2), added a second recruiting sub-station category (to separate large and small sub-stations) making 6 awards at that level, and added 2 individual awards bringing that total to 6. The new individual awards were rookie recruiter of the year, and a centurion award for outgoing recruiters who wrote at least 100 contracts during their tour of duty (maximum 48 months). A district awards board was added to select top district-level, and individual award recipients, i.e., the best in the district, while recruiting station commanders selected top recruiting-station-level recipients, i.e., the best in the station. Rather than using a point system (as in FY91), all but 2 categories calculated the percentage achieved as the standard for awards. For example the shipping mission category for units was calculated as follows:

$$\text{\# required , \# shipped = \% shipped}$$

The exceptions were net productivity and band contracts. The net productivity category was calculated as (gross contracts minus pool discharges) divided by (number of months times number of recruiters) equals monthly productivity average per recruiter. Band contracts were counted as the number shipped.

FY95. In this plan, the district added annual awards for a top overall recruiting station, rookie recruiter, and NCOIC. An award for any recruiter achieving 50 contracts was also added. A point system for recruiting stations was reinstituted, while recruiting sub-stations and individual recruiters retained the FY94 format. Recruiting station point calculations included 4 shipping criteria, 5 production criteria, and 5 recruiting station quality categories. All categories except evenflow shipping (calculated by time period) calculated points as 10 percent times the percentage of goal or standard achieved. No points were awarded for recruit quality, but points were deducted for not achieving quality standards. Points were also deducted for not achieving standards in recruiting station quality.

The FY95 plan also included a two-month campaign in late spring that counted contracts written by recruiters, NCOIC by unit size (large or small), and recruiting stations/sub-stations. To qualify, units were required to meet their monthly mission, and individuals were required to write at least two net new contracts per month. Those with the most contracts received district commander certificates of commendation and either a plaque for best in the district, or a desk set for first place in each recruiting station, or a mug for second place in each recruiting station.

9TH DISTRICT
Annual Plan

Unit Awards. The FY95 and FY96 annual plans reward each of the top three recruiting stations for monthly, quarterly, and annual achievement. Points are awarded for various shipping, contract, attrition and bonus categories. Recruit quality and quantity as well as regular timely shipping and contract submission standards are the focus of the plan. Awards are a Spearhead plaque for monthly winners, a Trident plaque for quarterly winners, and a 9mm replica pistol for annual winners.

Individual Awards. Individual recruiters are rewarded in three categories for contracts written as they are achieved. Additionally, awards based on net accessions per recruiter (APR), are presented by the district to the Sergeant Major of the month, district recruiter of the quarter, district recruiter of the year, district non-commissioned officer in charge (NCOIC) of the quarter, and district NCOIC of the year. Depending on the level of award and length of time to achieve the award (annual awards are usually more valuable than monthly awards), the awards range from certificates and plaques to Navy Achievement Medals.

Short-Term Campaigns

In the fall of FY95 and FY96, short-term campaigns were conducted for two months (four months for NCOICs). The FY95 campaign used a cowboy theme and concentrated on gross contracts written for individual recruiters and contract placement in six-month shipping pools for NCOICs. Recruits in DEP received awards for referrals to recruiters. Over 320 recruiter and 65 NCOIC awards were available and included shirts, model guns, and cowboy hats. One NCOIC was chosen as the top from all recruiting sub-stations based on the percentage of six-month pool achieved, and received a replica 1890s colt 45 pistol.

In FY96, the revised fall campaign was conducted around a football theme. In this campaign, each contract written by individual recruiters was worth one point. Those recruiters achieving 4, 7, and 9 points received t-shirts specified for their respective point category. In addition, medals, certificates, and meritorious masts were awarded, based on point ranking, among the top 50 recruiters. NCOIC award criteria were determined by each recruiting station. Recruiting stations were also authorized to award one Navy Achievement Medal, 3 Commanding General (region) Certificates of Commendation, and 4 Commander (district) Certificates of Commendation.

Accessions per recruiter were the criteria for recruiting station achievement. The campaign was conducted as a double elimination tournament that rewards recruiting stations that perform well early in the campaign. The recruiting stations are randomly assigned to a matrix after the first round (approximately one week), and recruiting stations with high gross accessions per recruiter are in one matrix level while low gross accessions per recruiter are in another level. The recruiting stations compete against each other in their assigned level for up to 8 rounds until one recruiting station emerges as the winner. District staff also competed in this campaign. They participated in a football pool by selecting individual winners and district total gross APR each round. The staff person with the most winning choices was the winner.

BIBLIOGRAPHY

GENERAL

Asch, B. J., and B. R. Orvis, *Recent Recruiting Trends and Their Implications: Preliminary Analysis and Recommendations*, RAND, MR-549-A/OSD, 1994.

Military Recruiting: More Innovative Approaches Needed, General Accounting Office, GAO/NSIAD-95-22, December 1994.

Murray, M., and L. McDonald, *Recent Recruiting Trends and Their Implications for Models of Enlistment Supply*, RAND, MR-847-OSD/A, 1997.

Orvis, B. R., N. Sastry, and L. L. McDonald, *Recent Recruiting Trends and Their Implications: Interim Report*, RAND, MR-677-A/OSD, 1995.

AIR FORCE

Mechanical GTEP - AI Shipper Incentive Program, Recruiting Service Headquarters, Message #950032, FY 95.

Operation ASAP, Recruiting Service Headquarters, Message #920148, 4/1/0/92

Recruiting Service Incentive Awards Program, ATC Regulation 900-18, 8/24/90, 3/18/91,3/27/92, 2/22/93.

Recruiting Service Incentive Awards Program, AETC Instruction 36-2804, 12/15/94.

Squadron Incentive Awards Programs, Air Force 360th Group, FY 93 - FY 95.

Squadron Recruiting Competition System and Incentive Awards Programs, Air Force 369th Group, FY 93 - FY 96.

Squadron Recruiting Competition System and Incentive Awards Programs, Air Force 367th Group, FY 93 - FY 96.

USAF Recruiting Service Competition System Rules-FY 88 to FY 93, and FY 95, FY 96 Squadron, Headquarters, United States Air Force Recruiting Service.

USAF Recruiting Service Squadron Competition System Rules-FY 95 & FY 96, Headquarters, United States Air Force Recruiting Service.

ARMY

Asch, B. J., and L. A. Karoly, *The Role of the Job Counselor in the Military Enlistment Process,* RAND, MR-315-FMP, 1993.

Berner, K., and T. Daula, "Recruiting Goals, Regime Shifts, and the Supply of Labor to the Army," *Defence Economics*, Vol. 4, No. 4, pp. 315-328, 1993.

Dertouzos, James N., comment by Matthew S. Goldberg, *Microeconomic Foundations of Recruiter Behavior: Implications for Aggregate Enlistment Models,* Army Manpower Economics, Ch. 4, Westview Press, Inc., 1986.

Dertouzos, James N., *Recruiter Incentive and Enlistment Supply*, RAND, R-3065-MIL, 1985.

Recruiting Incentive Awards messages, various years.

Success 2000, United States Army Recruiting Headquarters Memorandum, August 29, 1994 and September 21, 1994.

Success 2000 Memorandum, Information Paper, July 5, 1994.

United States Army Recruiting Command, Recruiting Edge Bulletins, September 1989 to 1st Quarter 1995.

United States Army Recruiting Command Regulation 672-10, various years, 1982 to 1989.

MARINES

Administrative and Issue Procedures for Decorations, Medals, and Awards, Commandant of the Marine Corps, MCO 1650.19F, MHM, November 15, 1993.

Depot Decorations and Awards Program, Western Recruiting Region, DepO 1650.7L, 1A, June 9, 1993.

Depot Decorations and Awards Program, Western Recruiting Region, DepO 1650.7M, 1A, Undated.

District 1 Recruiter Incentive Plans, Various District and Station Plans, FY 91 to FY 96.

District 4 Recruiter Incentive Plans, District and Station Plans, FY 96.

District 6 Recruiter Incentive Plans, Various District Plans, FY 94, FY 96.

District 8 Recruiter Incentive Plans, Various District Plans, FY 87 to FY 96.

District 9 Recruiter Incentive Plans, District Plans, FY 84, FY 95, FY 96.

District 12 Recruiter Incentive Plans, Various District and Station Plans, FY 91 to FY 96.

Marine Corps Promotion Manual, Volume 2, Enlisted Promotions, MCO P1400.32A, MMPR-2, December 21, 1989.

Navy and Marine Corps Awards Manual, Secretary of the Navy, SECNAVINST 1650.1F, OP-09B33, August 8, 1991.

Personal Awards, Commanding General Marine Corps Recruiting Command, MCRCO 1650.1A, A, January 22, 1996.

Personnel Procurement Operations Plan (OPLAN), Commandant of the Marine Corps, FY 87, 1050 MRRE, September 1987

Personnel Procurement Operations Plan (OPLAN), Commandant of the Marine Corps, FY 88 - FY 93, 1100 MRRP, each September from 1988 - 1992.

Personnel Procurement Operations Plan (OPLAN), Commanding General of the Marine Corps Recruiting and Recruit Training Command, FY 94 & FY 95, 1100 MRRP, each September from 1993 - 1994.

Rewards and Recognition FY 96, Eastern Recruiting Region, 1100 RCTG, September 14, 1995.

Superior Performance Award FY 95, Eastern Recruiting Region, DepBul 1650, RCTG.

Triple Crown War Club Award FY 96, Eastern Recruiting Region, 1650 RCTG, February 15, 1996.

Volume III, Guidebook for Recruiting Station Operations, Book 1 (Chapters 1 - 6), Book 2 Chapters (7-10), July 1984.

Volume V, Planning and Management Guide for District Recruiting Operations and Support Procedures, Book 1 (Chapters 1 - 4), Book 2 (Chapters 5-8), March 1990.

Volume I, Guidebook for Recruiters, Commandant of the Marine Corps, 1130 MRRT, August 12, 1993.

NAVY

Asch, Beth J., *Navy Recruiter Productivity and the Freeman Plan,* RAND, R-3713-FMP, 1990.

Barfield, L. C., *An Analysis of Enlisted Navy Recruiter Productivity and Incentive Programs, FY 1988 - FY 1990,* Naval Postgraduate School, September 1993.

Briggs, Lieutenant, *Quality Incentive System Weights*, Commander Navy Recruiting Command, Research Studies Branch of the Research Division, November 1994.

CNA Support of the Metcalf Study: A Study of Navy Recruiting, Center for Naval Analyses, Briefings Slides 89 -1302 and 89 - 2261, June and October 1989.

Cooke, Timothy, *Geographic Variation in Recruiter Productivity,* Center for Naval Analyses, Research Memorandum 88-21, February 1988a.

Cooke, Timothy, *Recruiting Resources and Policy,* Center for Naval Analyses, CRM 88-27, May 1988b.

Cooke, Timothy, *Indicators of Navy Recruiting Success: A Review of Recruiting Issues and Evidence,* Center for Naval Analyses, Center for Naval Analyses, Research Memorandum 87-58, May 1987a.

Cooke, Timothy, *Recruiting Efficiency and Enlistment Objectives,* Center for Naval Analyses, Research Memorandum 87-181, September 1987b.

Cooke, Timothy, *Cost Saving Changes in the Number of Recruiters: Recent Navy Experience,* Center for Naval Analyses (CNA)87-1601, August 1987c.

Enlisted Recruiting Goaling Policies, Commander Navy Recruiting Command Note *1133*, FY 84 to FY 95.

Gold Wreath Program (revised), excerpted from Navy Recruiting Command Instruction 1650.4K, change order 2, effective 3/28/94.

Jehn, Christopher, and William F. Shughart, *Recruiters, Quotas, and the Number of Enlistments,* Center for Naval Analyses, CNS 1073, December 1996.

Lerro, Pat, et al., *Navy Recruiting Planning for the Future,* Human Resources Research Organization, June 1989.

Navy Recruiting Command Competition System (NRCCS) Field Guide, Commander Navy Recruiting Command Instruction 1650.8G to 1650.8J, FY 87 to FY 90.

Navy Recruiting Command Individual and Unit Annual Incentive Awards, Navy Recruiting Command Instruction 1650.16D, March 15, 1994.

Recruiter Productivity and Personnel Management System "The Freeman Plan," Navy Recruiting Command.

Recruiter Meritorious Advancement Program (RMAP), Commander Navy Recruiting Command Instruction 1430.1, 1430.1A, 1430.1A Change 1 and 2, FY 90 - FY 92.

Recruiter Advancement Through Excellence (RATE) Program, Commander Navy Recruiting Command Instruction 1430.2, 1430.2 Change 1, 1430.2A, 1430.2A Change 1, 1430.2B, FY 92 - FY 94.

Recruiter Excellence Incentive Program (REIP), Commander Navy Recruiting Command Instruction 1430.4, 1430.4 Change 2, FY 94.